1

Where Do You Get Your Protein? Rethinking Food

Sharon Leontine Wallenberg

Liberty 61 Books

"Where Do You Get Your Protein? Rethinking Food"

Library of Congress Catalogue in Publication data

ISBN: 979-8-9882618-2-7

Liberty 61 Books

Dedication

This book is dedicated to all inhabitants of our home, planet Earth:

Those individuals seeking protein;

Those individuals seen as protein (and apparel, entertainment, test subjects, inferior individuals, and otherwise disposables); and

Those enlightened individuals who know protein comes from plants, and who have the courage to change the world, our precious home. planet Earth!

Acknowledgements

Ira J Raab, NYS Supreme Court Justice, Retired, for being a Wonderful Friend and for editing all my books.

Purpose

The purpose of this book is to offer proof that protein comes from plants, and that those individuals who obtain their protein from plants are not only equally healthy as those who do not, but often excel in physicality way beyond the many individuals relying on secondary protein. Additionally, guidance and support are offered to individuals seeking to obtain their protein from plants by adopting a plant-based lifestyle without being overwhelmed by mundane and boring details.

Introduction

This book is about protein, where it comes from, what happens when it is consumed. It also explores the history, mentality, and origins of food as well as the implications of diet on health. It hopes to encourage the Reader to experiment with the lessons learned, proactively explore, and experiment with imagination and courage. It strives to give the Reader a new view on an old topic.

This book is a food enlightenment book and not a cookbook. Before you close the book and walk away, take heart! Also included are many of your favorite foods made plant-based, as well as festive and decorative holiday cakes that are totally plant-based, gorgeous, and delicious. It has festive holiday menus, and guidance for eating out.

Additionally, it tells the facts behind the way we eat, who benefits and who does not, what the long-range outcomes are for ourselves, others, and the planet if we pursue obtaining our protein from the destructive SAD (Standard American Diet).

Contents

1: Where Do You Get Your Protein?

2: Photosynthesis; The Source of All Protein

3: What the Experts Say About Protein

4: Sugar – Empty Calories Not Diabetes Or Other NCDs

5: Carbohydrates – "Good" Carbs and "Bad Carbs"

6: Fat and Cholesterol Are Not What You Think

7: Anything Else? Vitamins, Minerals, Fiber, Microbes

8: Meet The Vegan Athletes

9: Protein: Winners and Losers

10: Understanding Zoonotic Disease

11: Earth's Limited Resources

12: Dairy Is Scary

13: Eggs – A Good Source of Cholesterol, Not "Protein"

14: Meet Your Bacon

15: Animal Ag Source of 'Protein' or Impending Disaster?

16: Meet The Sea Individuals

17: Food's Humble Beginings: Creativity, Resourcefulness, Imagination

18: Raw Food for Strength and Endurance

19: Adventures in Produce Shopping

20: A Field Trip To The Supermarket

21: Breakfast: The Beginning

22: Soup First

23: Salads: Verdant and Versatile

24: What's For Lunch?

25: Dinner: An Adventure in Innovation and Imagination

26: Herbs and Spices: The Little Giants

27: Cooking Basics: Steam, Broil, Sautee

28: Around The World Without Leaving The Kitchen

29: The Three Sisters, Ancient Wisdom for the Digital Age

30: The Four Seasons

31: Dessert - Elegant Endings

32: Holiday Menus

33: Baking - Yes You Still Can!

34: Agriculture: Conventional, Organic, and Veganic

35: Let's Eat Out!

36: My Vegan Kitchen

37: Conclusion

Glossary

Antioxidants - compounds that inhibit oxidation, a chemical reaction that can produce free radicals and chain reactions that may damage the cells of organisms. It is in substances such as vitamin C or E and removes potentially damaging oxidizing agents in a living organism.

MMA - Mixed Martial Arts sometimes referred to as cage fighting, no holds barred, and ultimate fighting, and originally referred to as Vale Tudo is full contact combat sport based on striking, grappling and ground fighting, incorporating techniques from various combat sports from around the world.

NASM - National Academy of Sports Medicine an American fitness training provider founded in 1987. Its headquarters is in Gilbert Arizona.

NCD – Non-Communicable Diseases including Heart Disease, Diabetes, some cancers, overweight and obesity which are linked to the meat and dairy diet.

Photosynthesis the process by which green plants and some other organisms use sunlight to synthesize foods from carbon dioxide and water. Photosynthesis in plants generally involves the the green pigment chlorophyll and generates oxygen as a byproduct.

Selenium - a photosensitive element that occurs in both crystalline and amorphous forms. It is an essential component of various enzymes and proteins, called selenoproteins, that help to make DNA and protect against cell damage and infections, these proteins are also involved in reproduction and the metabolism of thyroid hormones.

Synthesize – to make something or combine a number of different pieces into a whole.

Chapter 1: Where Do You Get Your Protein?

We begin our adventure of exploring PROTEIN!

Elephants are the strongest animal in the world. They eat leaves.

Horses are one of the fastest animals in the world. They eat grass.

Animals raised for human food would also eat some form of vegetation in their natural environment.

Vegan Athletes comprise the minority of athletes according to GreatVeganAthletes.com, and yet win the majority of competitions! Why? Because they get their PROTEIN FROM PLANTS!

Food has three categories: Protein, Carbohydrates, and Fat. All three are essential for life. The human body also requires vitamins, minerals, and fiber for optimal good health. The Whole Food Plant Based Diet contains all of these without unnecessary and harmful additional fat, cholesterol, antibiotics, hormones, and harmful microbes in the meat and dairy based diet.

Protein provides the functional and structural components of the human body, and the synthesis of hormones and neurotransmitters. Digestion breaks down protein into amino acids, which are then used by the body.

Amino acids are categorized as essential, conditionally essential, or nonessential. There are 22 amino acids, only eight of these amino acids are considered essential. They are: histidine, isoleucine, lysine, methionine, phenylalanine, threonine, tryptophan, valine, methionine, and phenylalanine. The amino acid arginine is considered essential when fighting cancer.

Essential amino acids are organic. In Chemistry, compounds that contain carbon, hydrogen, nitrogen, and oxygen are classified as organic, and those that do not contain carbon are classified as inorganic. Amino acids contain carbon, nitrogen, hydrogen, and oxygen, along with a variable side chain group. Essential amino acids cannot be made by the body. They must be obtained by diet. Plants are the primary source of essential amino acids. Animals, who get their own protein from plants, are a secondary source of protein.

There is sufficient protein in vegetables and fruit, especially in the traditional combination of grains and legumes which contains all the essential amino acids, for humans to survive and flourish.

Beans belong to a family of high-protein plant foods called legumes. Although different beans provide varying amounts of nutrients, they all contain a similar balance of essential amino acids. Black beans and kidney beans contain concentrations of all essential amino acids. All beans are a good source of lysine. Beans provide all nine essential amino acids except methionine.

Grains are generally high in methionine. Grains include rice, corn, oats, wheat, and quinoa. The bean and grain combinations are traditionally rice and beans or corn and lima beans.

Both the successful vegan athletes and the strong and fast animals all prove that the best source of protein is plants.

Chapter 2
Photosynthesis –
The Source of All Protein

"All energy comes from the sun" Thomas Edison.

The sun not only provides energy to produce electricity, but also provides solar energy for plants, animals, and humans, too. The process by which sunshine becomes food energy is the called "photosynthesis" and it is the beginning of protein.

The green color in plants, leaves, and grass is from chlorophyll, a pigment present in all plants. Chlorophyll absorbs sun light and uses it in photosynthesis, the process by which green plants and other organisms convert light energy from the sun into chemical energy. This energy can later be released as fuel for the organism's activities. During photosynthesis, food from sun light, carbon dioxide and water is synthesized, and oxygen is generated as a by-product. This is the basis of food energy.

During photosynthesis, vitamins, carbohydrates, amino acids (the building blocks of proteins), lipids (fats), and other components are synthesized. These are stored in the plant's leaves, stems, roots, fruits, grains, tubers, and legumes. Minerals from the ground the plants grow in supply the elements of nitrogen, phosphorus, sulfur, also required to form compounds.

Plants synthesize the wide range of vitamins that are essential for life. But unlike the other vitamins, Vitamin D from the sun is synthesized in the body.

Most animals, such as the horse, one of the world's fastest animals, and the elephant, one of the world's strongest animals, eat grass and leaves which are rich in energy synthesized from the sun. Animals raised for food, such as cattle and chickens, in nature, also eat foods rich in plant-based energy synthesized from the sun.

Why is it that some people believe they must eat animals, birds, eggs (a bird's menstrual cycle), and dairy (a mother cow's milk for her own baby calf), for protein instead of just going right to the source of protein, and eating plants?

Second-hand protein, obtained from eating other sentient individuals and their secretions, contains cholesterol, fat, hormones, antibiotics, often fecal matter, and other harmful microbes. The plant-based diet is rich in fiber which is absent in the meat and dairy based diet. Fiber facilitates the removal of toxic materials and excess hormones and is totally absent in the meat and dairy based diet.

The best source of protein comes from the sun and is found in plants. That is where vegans get their protein!

Chapter 3
What the Experts Say About Protein

Here is what some of the medical the experts are saying about PROTEIN:

Neal Barnard, M.D., Founder of Physicians Committee For Responsible Medicine (PCRM): "Myth: You Can't Get Enough Protein on a Vegan Diet. This myth will not die, despite (1) statements supporting vegan diets from major nutrition organizations, (2) the wealth of protein in beans, vegetables, and grains, (3) the massive musculature of rhinoceroses, elephants, and other vegan animals, and (4) the millions of people following vegan diets with no evidence that protein is an issue at all."

John A. McDougall, M.D.: "Nature designed and synthesized our foods complete with all the essential nutrients for human life long before they reach the dinner table. All the essential and nonessential amino acids are represented in single unrefined starches such as rice, corn, wheat, and potatoes in amounts in excess of every individual's needs, even if they are endurance athletes or weight-lifters."

Before making any important decision in life, one of the most important considerations is always the results. Will I get the results I am looking for? If you not only want to be healthy, but also be in your best possible shape, consider what these exceptional individuals, vegan athletes, are saying about protein:

The list of successful plant-based vegan athletes also includes Venus Williams, Professional Tennis Player, and many, many others. These individuals are not only exceptional because of their health, stamina, accomplishments, choice of compassionate diet, but also their courage and inner strength. For example, consider just one of many outstanding athletes – Seba Johnson. This is her story:

Seba Johnson is the first Black woman Olympic skier, and youngest Alpine Ski Racer in Olympic History! In the 1988 Winter Olympics in Calgary she placed 28th out of 64 of the world's best in the Women's Giant Slalom at age 14. She received death threats, hate mail, and attempts to disrupt her safety then, and through the following World Cup and World Alpine Ski Championship competitions. Skiing was considered a White man's sport.

Seba was born in St. Croix, US Virgin Islands. She lived in a public housing project, and attended Head Start. Her family moved around, living in New Hampshire, Maine, and Nevada. A vegan since birth, Seba learned about animal exploitation and she attended protests with her Mother. By her early teens, she held her own protests, once standing alone with a handmade sign outside a zoo.

In the 1992 Winter Olympic Games in Albertville, France, Seba qualified for the 1994 Games in Lillehammer, Norway. She boycotted them because Norway had resumed commercial hunting for whales. Seba was disqualified from a World Cup ski race for refusing to wear a ski suit with a patch of leather on it.

"We must connect to a moral and ethical regard for each human and nonhuman animal until oppression is completely eradicated." Seba Johnson.

Chapter 4
Sugar – Empty Calories Not Diabetes Or Other NCDs

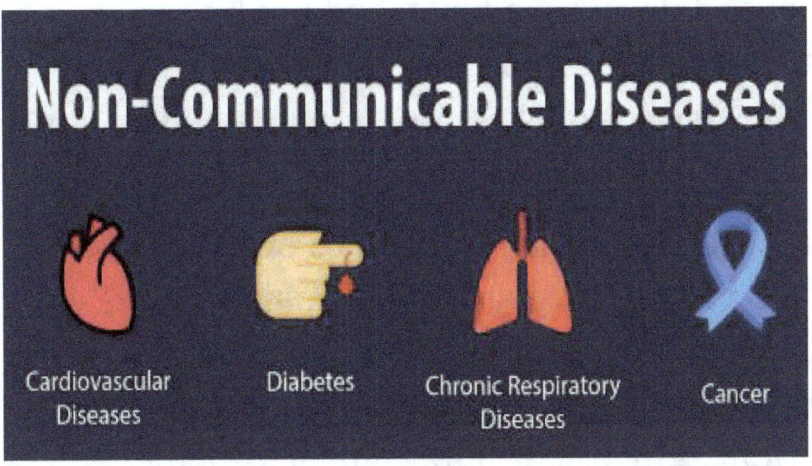

Why is the first question audiences ask me is always about 'sugar'?

My assumption is that these people are concerned about diabetes. I could eat a bowl of sugar a day, which I would never do, and still not get diabetes. Table sugar is processed. That means the vitamins, minerals, fiber and nutrition originally there in nature is gone, and only the calories remain. This is why sugar is referred to as 'empty calories'.

Sugar is not the cause of diabetes. Diabetes is caused by the fat and cholesterol in the meat and dairy based diet, and not by sugar. This fat fills the body's cells and makes it impossible for glucose from digestion to enter and nourish the cells.

The digestive system processes everything that is eaten into smaller and smaller pieces and adds digestive enzymes. The end-product of digestion is the smallest molecule possible, glucose, a simple sugar which is absorbed directly into the blood stream through the villi. These are small finger like projections in the intestines. Inside each villus is a network of blood vessels called capillaries. They have very thin walls and pick up the smallest molecule of digested food - glucose. This single molecule, glucose, the end-product of digestion, is absorbed directly into the blood stream and nourishes every cell in the body.

When glucose circulating throughout the body to nourish every cell, is unable to enter cells due to excessive fat and cholesterol in the cells, it remains in the bloodstream and causes a symptom of diabetes. That is why there is excess sugar in the blood and urine of people with diabetes. Eating sugar free foods will do nothing to change this. It will only put you at risk for the side effects of sugar substitutes. This excess glucose is removed from the blood by the kidneys and is excreted in urine causing the symptoms of diabetes.

Glucose is the energy source that powers everything including thoughts. When cells are deprived of glucose for energy, fatigue occurs. The glucose that cannot enter the cells, because they are filled with fat, remains in the bloodstream and becomes very concentrated. It requires copious amounts of water to excrete the excess glucose causing dehydration. Weight loss can occur indicating the cells are starving.

Type two diabetes is diagnosed when a Doctor takes a blood sample and finds an unusually high level of glucose, the patient experiences fatigue, is losing water rapidly, and has excessive thirst.

There are two types of diabetes. Type one diabetes, also called childhood onset diabetes, and insulin dependent diabetes, is less common than type two diabetes. It is usually diagnosed in childhood and is invariably treated with insulin. Type one diabetes occurs when the immune system attacks and destroys the insulin producing cells in the pancreas.

Genes are not solely responsible for this phenomenon. Identical twins prove this. Often one twin has type one diabetes and the other twin does not have diabetes at all. *Studies prove that type one diabetes is caused by a reaction to cow's milk in infants and young children.* Unlike people with type two diabetes, people with type one diabetes always need insulin. However, diet and lifestyle changes can keep insulin doses to a minimum and reduce the risk of complications.

Insulin is a hormone that is produced in the pancreas and is released into the blood stream where it travels to various cells in the body. Like a key sliding into a lock, insulin attaches to a receptor on the cell's surface and allows glucose to enter. Diabetes occurs when insulin cannot get the cell to allow the glucose inside. This is called insulin resistance. There is nothing wrong with the insulin, the glucose, or the cell. The problem is the cell's refusal to allow the glucose in because something is already in the cell occupying the space needed by the glucose. That something is fat. These traces of fat begin to accumulate many years before diabetes manifests.

Normally, fat is burned by mitochondria, little furnaces in the cells, for use as fuel for energy to power muscle cells. Studies prove that as fat in cells increases, mitochondria avoid burning it, as if to save it for future use. Reducing fat in the diet has been proven to reduce the fat in the cells which has been preventing the absorption of glucose, causing sugar in the blood stream, and thus eliminating one of the symptoms of diabetes.

Diabetic patients are asked to avoid sugar and starchy foods because they break down into sugar in the digestive tract. However, starchy foods are prevalent in diets in Japan, China, Thailand, and other parts of Asia and Africa where diabetes is rare. When people from these countries move to Europe or North America, where diabetes, heart disease, cancer and obesity, also known as the Non-Communicable Diseases (NCDs) are prevalent, they change to a meat and dairy based diet, and their incidences of diabetes and the other NCDs skyrocket.

People living in countries where the traditional diet is vegetables, rice, and beans do not get diabetes. When people from these cultures move to countries where meat and dairy is the preferred diet, or if the traditional diet in these countries changes to the more affluent meat and dairy diet, their incidence of diabetes skyrocket. This is what is currently happening in Mexico.

Hemoglobin is the pigment that gives color to red blood cells. Glucose enters red blood cells and sticks to hemoglobin. An A1c test shows how much glucose is stuck to the hemoglobin. Research shows that A1c values should be below 7% or better yet – 6.5%. The American Dietetic Association diet reduced A1c by 0.4%, but the plant-based vegan diet was three times more effective reducing A1c by an average of 1.2%. The vegan diet also reduced body weight and cholesterol. Studies show that a one point drop in A1c lowers the risk of eye and kidney complications by 37%.

The plant-based vegan diet is the only scientifically proven way to prevent, control, and reverse diabetes. It can reverse type two diabetes, and control type one diabetes, keeping medications to a minimum. It has nothing to do with sugar!

Diabetes is one of the Non-Communicable Diseases (NCDs) according to the United Nations World Health Organization. The NCDs also include Heart Disease, Cancer, and Obesity. All result from a diet of second hand protein from meat, poultry, fish, seafood, dairy and eggs. According to the United Nations World Health Organization (WHO), all NCDs can cause mortality and morbidity.

Heart disease is the leading cause of death for both men and women in the United States today. Heart disease results when the coronary arteries which bring blood and oxygen to the heart start to narrow, pinching off blood flow, and threatening the viability of the heart. Arteries narrow due to the growth of small, raised areas, or plaques on the inside of the arteries preventing normal blood flow. These plaques are composed of cholesterol and fat, from meat, poultry, fish, and dairy. The human body produces enough of its own cholesterol. Additional cholesterol from eating secondary protein instead of getting protein from plants, ultimately restricts blood flow causing heart disease, strokes, erectile dysfunction, and other morbidities. Fortunately, a plant-based vegan diet has been proven to prevent and reverse heart disease.

The Framingham Heart Study has spent many decades tracking who gets heart attacks and who doesn't. Among its key findings is that the lower the cholesterol, the lower the risk of heart problems. While some authorities consider 200 mg/dl to be the boundary between desirable levels and high levels, the Framingham Study showed that a level lower than 200 is actually better. In decades of research, not a single person in the Framingham Study with a cholesterol level below 150 had a heart attack.

Cholesterol is a raw material made in the cells of all sentient beings, including humans. It is used to make cell membranes and hormones, including testosterone and estrogen. It is inserted into the thin cell membranes that surround each cell in the body, and it acts as a glue to hold membranes together. The liver sends cholesterol particles into the bloodstream for these uses.

The best way to avoid or reverse diabetes and heart disease is by getting your 'protein' from plants, not animals!

What about cancer? Your best defense against cancer is prevention. Cancer is currently the second leading cause of death in the developed world. Cancer starts deep within the cells of the body. In the cell, biological and chemical interactions occur constantly. Cells work hard to control the use of oxygen and various nutrients, communicate messages, create new substances, and build new cells. The trillions of cells in the body communicate, remove toxic substances, repair injured cells, and prevent cells with damaged genetic material from reproducing.

Cancer begins when something goes wrong in a cell. The genetic blueprint, or DNA, deep inside a cell's nucleus can become damaged. When thus impaired, a cell multiplies out of control and forms a tumor. The tumor eventually invades healthy tissues and spreads to nearby tissues. Cancer cells can enter the blood stream and metastasize, invade other organs or parts of the body.

Carcinogens, cancer-causing chemicals found in certain foods and tobacco, can damage the DNA in cells. Certain foods block carcinogens from entering cells and damaging DNA or limit the damage that occurs. Even at later stages, out of control cell multiplication can be reduced or prevented. The mineral selenium in whole grains, and the brightly colored carotenoids found in vegetables and fruits have shown the ability to slow or stop cancer growth. Folic acid found in leafy greens, oranges, and legumes has also been proven to protect DNA.

Oxygen is fundamental to life. Yet some of this essential substance can become unstable and cause serious problems in the body. Chemical reactions can leave oxygen with too many electrons, making it a 'free radical'. Free radicals are highly reactive molecules looking for other molecules to react with. When they attack DNA inside cells, the cells can begin multiplying out of control, which is the beginning of cancer. Meats, especially ones that contain nitrates, feed free radicals. Antioxidants, which plant-based diets are rich in, keep free radicals in check, and protect DNA against carcinogens.

Researchers have studied people with cancer, and those seemingly protected from it. Studies have confirmed that genes are not the cause of cancer. Rather, eating habits, smoking, and drinking habits determine vulnerability to cancer. Obtaining your 'protein' from a plant-based, rather than a meat and dairy based diet can prevent cancer or alter its course once it has been diagnosed.

Cancers most commonly occur where there is a continual turnover and division of cells. The most vulnerable areas are where old cells are continually sloughed off and new ones built including the skin, lungs, and digestive tract; and in organs that secrete substances, the breast; and in organs of reproduction: the uterus, ovaries, and testes. Scientific research can link the relationship between animal 'protein' and plant 'protein' in causing and preventing these cancers.

In hundreds of research studies, scientists have tracked how cancer rates differ among groups of people whose genetic backgrounds are similar, but their diets are different. A direct relationship between diet and cancer risk emerged. The people who eat more fruit, vegetables, and whole grains, and avoid meat, dairy and fatty foods have a much lower cancer risk. They take advantage of certain protective nutrients while avoiding risky foods. If cancer does develop, the dietary characteristics of the plant-based vegan diet tend to improve survival.

Breast cancer in Japan was rare, according to research conducted there, and if Japanese women did get breast cancer, it was usually less aggressive than breast cancer in American women, and they were more likely to survive. Their traditional diet has plenty of rice and vegetables, and very little meat or dairy products. People who moved from Japan to the United States changed their traditional plant based "protein" for meat and dairy "protein". This caused their breast cancer rates to more than triple, and prostate cancer to become almost five times as common.

Between 1975 and 2000, fast-food chains started to crop up in Japan, featuring hamburgers, chicken, and cheese, and breast cancer incidence doubled. The problem was not polluted water or radiation. The problem was food. A 2016 study found that Japanese women who had Westernized their diets the most had an 83 percent higher breast cancer risk, compared with those who had stayed with more traditional eating habits. The same phenomenon has been shown in other countries: As meat and dairy "protein" pushes plant-based "protein" off the plate, cancer rates rise.

Dairy affects the odds of surviving breast cancer. A California study of women diagnosed with breast cancer found that those women consuming one or more servings of whole fat dairy products: milk, butter, cheese, yogurt, ice cream, etc., per day had a 50 percent increased risk of dying from their cancer over the twelve years of the study, as compared with those women who avoided all dairy.

Fat intake was tested in the Women's Intervention Nutrition Study which included 2,437 women previously treated for breast cancer. Some women were asked to begin a low-fat diet, and the others continued their usual diets. After five years, the risk of cancer recurrence was reduced by 24 percent in the low-fat group. To avoid excess fats, the first step is to stop eating animals for "protein" in dairy products and meat. This will adjust the hormone levels and reduce the risk of cancer.

Fiber from vegetables and fruit is essential in combating cancer. This was tested in the Women's Healthy Eating and Living Study. The goal was not to prevent cancer, but rather to help 3,109 women who already had been treated for breast cancer. Half of the women were asked to have five fruit and vegetable servings each day, and the other half were asked to have eight servings of fruits and vegetables, plus 16 ounces of vegetable juice each day.

Researchers found that in the eight-a-day group, fiber intake rose from 22 to 29 grams per day, and fat intake fell from 28 percent of calories to 21 percent within the first year. In addition, estrogen and serum estradiol concentrations fell, as well. This proves that changing your diet from animals for "protein" to plants for "protein" can change your hormone levels, reduce your risk of having cancer, and increase your survival rate if you already have cancer.

In both men and women, soy cuts cancer risk. Soybeans contain isoflavones, which have a chemical structure that is similar to testosterone in men and estrogen in women. In test tube experiments, soy has been shown to attach to estrogen receptors. That led some initially to speculate that soy products might cause cancer. However, studies show the opposite. Women who consume the most soy products have about 30 percent lower risk of developing breast cancer, compared with their soy-avoiding friends.

Prostate cancer has been proven to be linked to dairy 'protein'. Two large Harvard studies tested the connection and found that milk-drinking men are much more likely to develop prostate cancer, compared with men who avoid dairy products. The Physicians' Health Study involved 20,885 men and found that those who had at least two and a half dairy servings per day had a 34 percent increased risk of developing prostate cancer. The second study, the Health Professionals Follow-up Study, included 47,781 men and found that men drinking more than two milk servings of dairy per day were 60 percent more likely to develop prostate cancer. The results of eleven different studies were combined, and showed that men consuming milk products have a 43 percent higher risk of dying from prostate cancer, compared with men who avoided dairy products.

Testicular cancer is one of the most common cancers in men. Dairy products, especially cheese, has been identified as a causation in many of the studies. A 2003 study showed that men who eat cheese had an 87 percent higher risk of developing testicular cancer compared with men who do not eat cheese. All dairy contains hormones, including estrogen, but they are more concentrated in cheese. Processed meats including sausage, bacon, turkey bacon, ham, and hot dogs are also linked to higher risk.

Hormones which speed the growth of cancer are especially plentiful in all dairy products including milk, yogurt and ice cream. Calcium from dairy does not benefit bones. According to the 1997 Nurses' Study at Harvard, milk drinkers broke more bones than people who avoid dairy. Many vegetables are excellent sources of calcium without the negative side effects of hormone rich milk.

The immune system is the body's first anticancer defense. Specialized white blood cells seek out and destroy cancer cells. Their strength depends on food supplying plenty of antioxidants, Vitamin C, fiber, carotenoids and omega fatty acids from flaxseed, canola oil, walnuts, and butternuts, and not from mercury and toxin ladened fish and fish oils.

If you are undergoing cancer treatment, the right foods for "protein" will support the healing process. Surgery and other treatments are essential. Healthful "protein" is also essential. Cancer cells can lurk in the body for years. Plant-based "protein" exercise, and other lifestyle practices, will help prevent cancer and be an invaluable aid in treating any cancer already in progress.

Remember, "protein" from meat, chicken, eggs, milk, dairy products, fish and seafood is high in cholesterol, carcinogens and hormones which speed the growth of abnormal cells and contains no fiber which is necessary for eliminating excess hormones and toxic substances to combat cancer. The plant-based diet by comparison, is high in "protein", contains antioxidants - protective nutrients which prevent cancer, and fiber which facilitates the removal of carcinogens and toxins.

Overweight and obesity, also known as a Non-Communicable Diseases (NCD), resulting from excessive fat and cholesterol in the secondary "protein" diet are leading causes of death and disability. This is according to the United Nations World Health Organization (WHO) European Regional Obesity Report, published by the WHO European Office for the Prevention and Control of Noncommunicable Diseases (NCDs). The report contains country-specific data from the 53 WHO European Member States and reveals that overweight and obesity increase the risk for many other non-communicable diseases, including cancer, cardiovascular diseases, type two diabetes, mellitus and chronic respiratory diseases. Two-thirds of adults in the WHO European Region, and one in three school-aged children, are living with overweight or obesity. The meat and dairy based diet for "protein" is the source of the fat and cholesterol which causes overweight and obesity. "Protein" from the low fat, high fiber plant-based diet is the antidote to this often life-threatening health dilemma.

Both the meat-based and plant-based diets supply plenty of "protein". There is as much protein in a serving of lentils, beans, tofu, soy milk, veggie burger, or similar meat substitute, as there is in a similar size serving of beef, chicken, fish, milk, cheese, or eggs. The difference is the saturated fat, cholesterol, hormones, antibiotics, harmful bacteria, chemicals, violence and injustice in meat and dairy "protein" versus the vitamins, minerals, antioxidants, and fiber in peaceful, sustainable plant-based "protein".

In conclusion, the reality is not that "sugar" is 'bad", and "protein" is "good", but that meat, dairy, poultry, eggs, fish and seafood are "bad" and fruit and vegetables are "good". A novel idea, I realize, but it is a scientific and empirical reality.

Chapter 5
Carbohydrates:
"Good" Carbs and "Bad" Carbs

"Good Carbs" and "Bad Carbs"

The so called "bad carbs" refers to processed foods. These are foods in boxes and bags which have been stripped of most of their protein, fiber, vitamins and minerals. These are also called "empty calories" because processed food contains calories, but none of the other necessary nutrients. All food in a box or a bag is processed. Unprocessed food comes from fields and trees.

There are many myths about carbohydrate. Some people choose to avoid gluten, the protein found in wheat. Only one person in a hundred has celiac, the allergy to gluten.

Carbohydrates are considered fattening, but carbohydrates have only 4 calories per gram, compared with 9 for fats and oils. Weight gain comes from eating "carbs" in cakes, cookies and processed foods, and not the "carbs" in whole food carbohydrates from fruit, vegetables, grains, beans and legumes. The carbohydrates from fruit and vegetables, and not "protein", are the source of energy for the body.

The "good carbs", unprocessed fruits and vegetables, and not second-hand animal based "protein", should make up the majority of the healthful diet. Fruit and vegetables provide nourishment for strength and energy, and vitamins, minerals, and fiber for optimal health, without the empty calories in processed foods, or the unhealthy fat and cholesterol in the meat and dairy based diet.

Plant based carbs, the "good" carbs, are the most delicious and the most healthful!

Chapter 6:
Fat and Cholesterol
Are Not What You Think

Chronic Overweight and Obesity

Cholesterol is a white, waxy substance, not found in plants, that is produced by humans and other sentient beings for use in their body for cell repairs, hormones, and other functions. The human body produces enough of its own cholesterol for these purposes. Cholesterol is an essential compound of the membranes that coats all cells and is the basic ingredient of the sex hormones testosterone and estrogen.

When humans consume meat, poultry, fish, and other animal-based foods, such as dairy products and eggs, they take on excess amounts of cholesterol. Ironically, eating fat and cholesterol causes the human body to manufacture excessive amounts of cholesterol. This explains why vegetarians who eat oil, butter, cheese, milk, ice cream, donuts, and pastries develop coronary disease despite their avoidance of meat, chicken and fish.

The unnecessary additional fat and cholesterol in the human body resulting from eating a meat and dairy based diet, clogs arteries, causing heart disease; fills cells so they cannot accept glucose for energy causing diabetes; and also is considered to be responsible for some cancers.

According to Neal Barnard, M.D. in "The Vegan Starter Kit": "Animal products drive cholesterol levels skyward. First of all, meat, dairy products, and eggs contain cholesterol – with eggs at the top of the list-and roughly half of the cholesterol you eat ends up in your bloodstream. Much worse is the saturated "bad" fat in dairy products, meat and eggs. It stimulates your body to make extra cholesterol. Plants are just the opposite. They have very little saturated fat and are essentially cholesterol free."

Cholesterol in the foods you eat raises your cholesterol level. Animal products are the only significant source of cholesterol. Surprisingly it is found mainly in the lean portions of meat. Cholesterol is in a chicken breast, salmon filet and lean portions of meat along with the second hand "protein". Animals, their offspring, and secretions eaten as "protein" are the only significant source of cholesterol in the human diet. Cholesterol is not found in plants. Chicken and fish have essentially the same cholesterol as beef. A single egg has 213 mg of cholesterol, but you knew that. Plants do not contain any cholesterol. They only provide protein, carbohydrates for energy, vitamins, minerals, micronutrients and fiber for optimal health.

Fat is a form of energy storage for an individual's use in the event of a food shortage. It is not used unless there is food insecurity. Fat is normally burned up by mitochondria, little furnaces in the cells, to use as fuel for energy to power muscle cells. Studies prove that as fat in cells increases, the mitochondria avoid burning it, as if to save it for future use. Reducing fat in the diet has been proven to reduce fat in the cells.

Saturated fats are sometimes called "bad fats". Their name comes from the fact that the fat molecule is completely covered with hydrogen atoms — that is, "saturated" with them. If it is not covered with hydrogen atoms, it is called "unsaturated". Saturated fats stimulate your liver to make more cholesterol. Unsaturated fats do not do that. Saturated fats are solid at room temperature, like cooled bacon grease. Vegetable oils are liquid at room temperature, showing they are unsaturated fat. All fruit, vegetables, whole grains and beans are very low in fat overall, with absolutely no saturated fat or cholesterol.

The best way to lower your cholesterol and saturated fat is to avoid animal products. Dr. Dean Ornish did a study using a vegan diet to reverse heart disease. Some Doctors still recommend 'chicken and fish' diets, which are not very effective because they only lower the amount of cholesterol in your blood by about 5 percent. A typical plant-based vegan diet lowers your cholesterol by about 20 percent.

The unnecessary additional fat and cholesterol in the human body resulting from eating a meat and dairy based diet, clogs arteries, causing heart disease; fills cells so they cannot accept glucose for energy causing diabetes; and is considered to be responsible for some cancers.

Why would people who have their own source of cholesterol, their own fat, and rarely have food insecurity, want someone else's fat and cholesterol? Excess fat and cholesterol have been linked to heart disease, diabetes and some cancers, making them even less desirable. Second hand protein from meat and dairy also contains unwanted antibiotics and microbes. Shouldn't the quest for protein lead you right to the source - plants? The most healthful diet is the cholesterol free, delicious whole food, plant based vegan diet! And it is the original source of all protein!

Chapter 7
Anything Else?
Vitamins, Minerals, Fiber, Microbes

Vitamins are organic – they contain carbon,
hydrogen, oxygen and nitrogen. They are
synthesized by plants and bacteria. People
can make their own Vitamin D from
sunlight. Some vitamins come from human
bowel activity. There are sufficient vitamins
in the Plant Based diet to make vitamin
supplements unnecessary.

Minerals are inorganic; they do not contain carbon and come from the earth. Plants absorb them through their roots and store them in their roots, stalks, leaves and fruit.

Vitamins and minerals mostly come directly from soil, not through animals. Vitamins, both the fat-soluble vitamins A, D, and K, and water-soluble vitamins B and C, as well as minerals, are readily available in a varied plant-based diet. Using animals as a source of vitamins and minerals for humans is essentially obtaining the vitamins and minerals second hand from the prematurely deceased individuals who originally received the vitamins and minerals from plants.

Vitamin D comes from sunshine and can overcome depression without the need for medication. It is a scientific fact that sunshine produces a chemical reaction in the brain. The brain produces serotonin, a chemical that is a potent mood enhancer. There is a relationship between serotonin production and bright light, usually the sun, but it can also be from artificial light. Serotonin is a natural anti-depressant without the dangerous side effects of anti-depressant drugs. Some of these drugs have been linked to suicides. Conversely, the lack of sunshine has been scientifically proven to cause depression. People who spend most of their time indoors not only miss receiving Vitamin D from the action of sunlight on the skin, but also have a higher risk of depression.

Minerals come from the soil plants are grown in. If soil is repeatedly planted, it becomes depleted of minerals and there are fewer nutrients in the produce. The evidence of this is the lack of flavor and taste in produce. Sustainable or veganic agriculture allows soil to replenish by using nitrogen rich cover crops and plowing them under to replenish the soil. This is not done in either conventional or organic agriculture.

A good way to know if there is an ample supply of vitamins and minerals in your diet is to eat fruit and vegetables of a variety of colors. This will ensure you are receiving lots of vitamins and minerals.

Fiber is essential for optimal health. Fiber transports toxins out of the body through the colon. Without fiber, toxins remain in the colon where they putrefy. The uneliminated toxins are reabsorbed through the villi of the intestine directly into the blood stream. Then they circulate to every part of the body and poison it.

Dietary fiber is found only in the whole food plant-based diet. Fruit, vegetables, seeds, nuts, grains and legumes are nutrient dense, high in fiber, and provide an excellent source of vitamins, minerals and protein. Fiber not only aids in the elimination of toxins, but also improves cholesterol levels, lowers blood sugar levels and aids in weight loss or weight management.

What are microbes? They include bacteria - such as Escherichia coli, found in the intestines of all people and animals, and Salmonella, usually found in birds, and many others. They are viruses, including

Covid 19, and many others. They are Archaea, Fungi (yeasts ad molds), Algae, and Protozoa. Microbes are generally found in meat and dairy rather than fruit and vegetables. If microbes are in produce, it is because waste from animal slaughterhouses containing microbes was used as fertilizer. Slaughterhouse waste used as fertilizer transmits microbes and disease, unlike the healthful veganic method of agriculture which uses healthful nitrogen rich cover crops for fertilizer.

Conclusion: Eat fruit and vegetables, of all colors, especially ones that are veganic and not conventional or organic, for "protein", vitamins, minerals, and fiber.

Chapter 8
Meet the Vegan Athletes

ROBERT CHEEKE, Vegan Bodybuilder and Vegan International Advisory Board Member

If you don't believe protein comes from plants, let me introduce you to some of the Vegan Athletes who get all of their protein from plants! Here are only a few of them, many are courtesy of Great Vegan Athletes.com: **Front Cover:**

Robert Cheeke is an American Vegan Bodybuilder, a Vegan International Advisory Board Member, Motivational Speaker, Author and Activist who has written "Vegan Bodybuilding & Fitness: The Complete Guide to Building Your Body on a Plant-Based Diet", and "Shred It! Your Complete Guide to Burning Fat and Building Muscle on a Whole-Food, Plant-Based Diet", and "Plant-Based Muscle".

Mac Danzig is an American Vegan Mixed Martial Artist. He competed as a lightweight in several MMA promotions, including the Ultimate Fighting Championship, and won. He was recently featured in the acclaimed, "Forks Over Knives" documentary related to the book that was on the New York Times bestseller list. Once, the fight world virtually scoffed at Mac's vegan diet. Now he is considered a pioneer who was ahead of the times.

Budjargal Byambaa is a Mongolian Ultra Distance Runner and a Vegan International Advisory Board Member. He is a raw Vegan Ultradistance Runner who runs extreme distance events over several days. He covers enormous distances at impressive speeds. In 2013 Budjargal broke the 24-

hour national record for his home nation of Mongolia after completing 182 km, and he has completed the 10-day Sri Chinmoy race five times. He won it in 2017 (1189 km) and again in 2019 (1222 km). In 2019 Budjargal completed the Xiamen 6-day race, winning with a distance of 834 km. These races are the equivalent of 29 marathons.

A

Mirsad Abdakovic is a Vegan Extreme Distance Runner who competes internationally. In 1989, at age 15, he won a national championship in cross country running.

Calle Alexander is an American Vegan Ninja Warrior. The Ninja Warrior sport originated in Japan and consists of obstacle courses with increasing difficulty. Competitors are eliminated for failing to complete the obstacle courses or for running out of time. Calle has taken on some of the most difficult courses in American Ninja

Warrior and has reached the national finals on many occasions.

"Allie", aka "The Bunny", aka "Cherry Bomb", (born Laura Dennis) is a Canadian Vegan Wrestler who is currently signed to All Elite Wrestling. She is best known for her time in Impact Wrestling where she is a former two-time Impact Knockout Champion.

Nana Almeida is a Brazilian World Class Vegan Swimmer who has been successful in Brazil and internationally including the Olympics, continental competitions, and national competitions. She grew up in a sport-oriented family. Her father coached soccer and her brothers also enjoyed sports.

Stefhan Andersen is a Swedish national Vegan Triathlon Champion. He went vegan in 2007. His main motivation initially was simply not to get sick: "I had like 20 days/year that I could not train on because I had a cold or something." Going vegan changed that.

Ida Andersson is a Vegan Swedish National Level Rower who competed on teams at national and international levels. Ida started rowing in 2002 in Normandy, France, where she spent some time at the University. She loved the teamwork aspects of rowing as well as the extremely hard exercise involved.

Austin Aries, (Daniel Healy Solwold Jr.), is a Vegan World Champion Pro Wrestler who has won numerous World Titles. Austin made his debut in 2000 and by 2004 was competing in the Ring of Honor. He is known for a range of spectacular signatures. He is the author of "Food Fight: My Plant Powered Journey From Bingo Halls To The Big Time". He is currently signed to the Control Your Narrative wrestling promotion.

Unsal Arik is a Turkish Vegan Boxer who currently lives in Germany. He fights in the Super Welterweight Division. After he become a vegan, he won the IBF European Champion, WBU World Champion and GBU World Champion. He also won the

UBF European title twice, WBC Asia title and the BDB International title.

Itir Atadiyen is an extremely successful Vegan Mountain Runner and Sky Runner from Turkey. Itir runs long distance races from 10 km to marathon and beyond. Most races have brutal height gains, usually exceeding 1000 meters.

Larkyn Austman is a Vegan Figure Skater who won medals in national and international competitions including Bronze medals in both the 2017 International Challenge Cup and the 2018 Canadian Cup; a Gold medal in the 2013 Canadian Championships; and a Silver medal in the 2012 Canadian Junior National Competition.

Cam F. Awesome , formerly Lenroy Thompson, is a Vegan Super Heavyweight and Heavyweight American Amateur Boxer with numerous titles. At age 20, he won the 2008 USA National Championships in the Super Heavyweight division. He also won the US title in 2008, 2010, 2013 and

2014 and the Golden Gloves in 2009, 2011 and 2013 at Super Heavyweight. He is featured in the 2017 Netflix boxing documentary, 'Counter Puncher'. "I started boxing in 2005", he explained, "I wanted to lose weight and get into better shape."

B

Patrik Baboumian is a Vegan and holds the title "Strongest Man of Germany" in the 105 kg division and holds the world log lift record in the 105kg category 165 kg (364 pounds), as well as the German heavyweight log lift record 180 kg (396 pounds).

Paolo Barbom is an Italian Vegan Cyclist known for his long-distance cycling events. He competes in mountain biking and loves races of up to 24 hours. In 2016, Paolo placed second in the 24-hour Barbano Vicentino race. He took third in the Bellaria Igea Marina, also a 24-hour event.

Borja Ignacio Perez Batet is a Vegan Multisport Athlete from Spain who competes internationally. He competed in the European and World Duathlon Championships in the 30-34 age group World title in 2016, World and European Duathlon Championships, and World Age Group Duathlon Champion, and won the San Silvestre Vellcana Amateur 10k.

Dorothy Lee "Dotsie" Bausch is a Vegan American cyclist. She is an Olympic Silver medalist, Advocate, Speaker, the Executive Director of the Nonprofit, Switch4Good, and Founder of two other nonprofits.

Hector Bellerin is a Vegan Footballer from Spain, now in the United Kingdom. He started with the Barcelona youth team as an attacking winger, and played for Spain at U16, U17, U19, U21 and full international level. In 2011, at age 16 he signed with Arsenal in the English Premier League.

Zack Belknap from Eugene, Oregon, is a Vegan who holds a World Natural Bodybuilding Federation Pro-Card and is a National Academy of Sports Medicine Certified Personal Trainer. Zack was awarded a WNBF Pro Card after impressive performances at regional level. "My greatest achievements in bodybuilding have been winning my pro card in September 2018 and then winning my first pro show in April 2019".

Kim Best is a Vegan Strong Woman from Scotland, home of the Highland Games. Her debut competition was at Scotland's Strongest Woman in 2018. According to Kim, "I have suffered with IBS since I was a teenager and discovered that animal by-products were the main trigger. I realized after reducing my dairy intake that animal protein from meat was also causing an issue, whereby I ended up with extremely sore kidneys and back pain. I turned vegan for my health and after when I was looking for recipes and ways to get enough of each food group, I became more informed on how the animals are treated. I can't imagine ever turning back or understand why I even thought it was natural in the first place."

Rob Bigwood is a Vegan Arm Wrestler who started arm wrestling in 2000. After a tournament in 2002, Rob started feeling uncomfortable about eating meat and began to consider a vegan diet. Like many other people, Rob was led to believe that meat was an essential part of building strength. He discovered from personal experience that nothing could be further from the truth!

Tiarah Lue Blanco is a Vegan Filipino American professional surfer from San Clemente, California, and member of the American Surfing Team. In 2014, she won the NSSA Southwest Women's U18 Season She won the first-place gold medal at an International Surfing Association Open Women's World Surfing Championship, and the Surfing Prime America Women's U18 Season, as well as several other surfing tournaments.

Ivan Blazquez is a Vegan Certified Exercise Physiologist with a Master degree in Exercise Physiology, and is a pro natural physique competitor/bodybuilder and a competitive triathlete. He has held a coveted pro card in natural bodybuilding since 2009, and gradually transitioned to a vegan diet as he experienced benefits for both health and physical performance.

Pam Boteler is a Vegan retired Sprint Canoeist who made history as the first woman to compete in Canoe at the 2000 US National Sprint/Kayak Championships. When Pam started competitive sprint canoeing in 2000. women were banned from national championship events.

Brendon Brazier is a Canadian Vegan Ironman and Endurance Athlete, Author, and Vegan Advocate. He is both Half Ironman and Full Ironman Triathlete. Ironman consists of a 2.4-mile swim, 112-mile cycle, and 26.2-mile marathon. He won the Bigfoot Half Ironman course record twice and was Canadian 50K champion for several years. In addition, Brendon is the Author of "The Thrive Diet", "Thrive Fitness", and "Thrive Foods: 200 Plant-Based Recipes for Peak Health", and Creator of the Vega line of food products and supplements.

Anabelle Broadbent is a Vegan Long-Distance Runner, born in Puerto Rico, who has taken wins and set course records. She is a member of the Philadelphia Masters Track & Field, races for the Mid-Atlantic Association, and serves on the Long-Distance Running Committee of USA Track & Field, and the Puerto Rico Masters Association.

Amelia Brodka is a Vegan Polish American Professional Skateboarder, Coach, and President of Exposure Skate Organization. She is a two-time European Park Skateboarding Champion, and qualified to compete in the inaugural women's park event at the Olympic Games.

Marc-Olivier Brouillette is an American Vegan Football Player who played in the Canadian National Football League. Marc-Olivier joined the Montreal Alouettes in May 2010 and played 103 games as a Linebacker or Safety.

Karl Bruder is a Vegan Bodybuilder who won at the WABBA Grand Prix (2016), took

6th place at the Mr. Universe, and placed 4th at the PCA Physical Culture.

Mirko Buchwald is a Vegan and one of the most respected instructors of Goju Ryu Karate which he studied for 25 years. He is a 6th Degree Black Belt and chief instructor of the San Francisco Goju Ryu Karate Centre. Mirko became the British Karate champion at age 20 and retained the title for two years.

C

Ramona Adelle Cadogan is a 50-year-old Vegan Masters Weightlifter who competes nationally in the United States as well as internationally. She has won Gold and Silver at the Pan American Masters Championships. Ramona competes in the 63 kg Weightlifting category and also competed in Powerlifting.

Molly Cameron is a Vegan Racer who won the 2004 and 2011 Cross Crusade Single Speed Series. She has been Oregon State Champion twice. and rides for the Portland

Bicycle Studio in addition to achieving a large number of individual race victories in her career. According to Molly, "When I turned 15 or 16, I realized that I did not have to eat meat, so I stopped."

Alexandra Morgan Carrasco is a Vegan and an American Professional Soccer Player for the San Diego Wave of the National Women's Soccer League, the highest division of women's professional soccer in the United States. She is one of the most successful Women's Soccer Players of her generation both at the national and international levels. Alex started playing for the California Golden Bears while at University and was then drafted as the overall number one in 2011.

Wilson Chandler is a Vegan National Basketball Association Player who is recognized as an entertaining and effective player capable of making a great contribution to his team's performance. He currently plays with the Brooklyn Nets and previously played with the New York Knicks.

Greg Chappell is a retired Vegan Batsman who was a leading batsman of his time. He captained Australia for two periods, 1975-1977 and then again from 1979 until his retirement in 1984. He played in 87 test matches and recorded a batting average of 53.86.

Frans Claes is a Vegan Mountain Biker from Belgium who competes nationally and internationally. He is an established leading biker and has been Belgian Champion twice, once in 2015, and again in 2016. He was the overall winner at the Union Cycliste Internationale (UCI) World Series Marathon in 2017.

Joe 'Monk' Coleman is a Vegan Bodybuilder who started competing in his 40s against much younger competitors. Joe became a vegan after years of an unhealthy lifestyle. Joe changed his lifestyle to include meditation, plant-based diet, and exercise.

Mindy Colette is a popular Vegan Bodybuilder and animal activist.

Kelly Colobella is a Vegan who has played in women's semi-professional (full tackle) American football since 2000. She became a key team member of Utah Falcons and played in the US National League. She contended for the National Championship four times and won twice.

Julia Trezise-Conroy is a Vegan Powerlifter from New Zealand, recognized for some amazing lifts. She holds the national records in all three of the sub-52 kg lift categories and successfully competed in the IPL Drug-Tested World Championships in Atlanta, Georgia.

Michaela Copenhaver is an American Vegan Rower in the Lightweight division. She started rowing in 2003 and continued at Princeton University where she competed at two National Collegiate Athletic Association championships and one Intercollegiate Rowing Association championship. In her senior year, she set a Sprint course record and won an IRA silver medal as stroke seat of the lightweight varsity eight.

Catra Corbett is a Vegan Runner who ran more than 250 ultramarathons. She holds the overall record for men and women, and completed the John Muir Trail out and back twice, for a total of 424 miles. Catra also has the second-best all-time result for a woman running one way, 212 miles.

Veronique Cormier is a Vegan Canadian Powerlifter who competes in the 57 kg category. At age 18, she competed in the Eastern Canadian Championships. At age 20, she hit the nationals in the Junior class and lifted a total of 312 kg. She then went on to the Pan American Championships later that year.

Vicky Cosionis a Vegan Tennis Player, now in her 40's, who started playing tennis in high school and has never taken lessons. She plays in the 'open' division, which is the highest non-professional level. There are no age divisions, and includes tennis teachers, retired professionals, college players and elite juniors.

Zak Covalcik is a Vegan Track Cyclist competing at the national level in the United States. He won twenty-six medals at the Elite National level, and has been Oregon State Champion ten times, as well as United States National Champion five times. He also successfully raced in Germany, Tasmania and Trinidad and Tobago.

Bradie Crandall from the United States is a Vegan Powerlifter. He reached international standards quickly, and by 2021 he raw benched 155 kg (342 pounds) in the 100 kg (220 pounds) category. He also deadlifted 280 kg (617 pounds) in the 100 kg (242 pounds) category.

Alison Crowdus is a Vegan Powerlifter from Northern Kentucky, United States, who qualified for the Xtreme Powerlifting Competition Finals at the Arnold Sports Festival, where she made her debut in March 2017. She is one of the few women in the world to have ever benched 500 pounds (227 kg).

Ana Cufer is Vegan Runner from Slovakia who is in the most demanding discipline, mountain running. She represented Slovakia in numerous international events and set several course records, among many other accomplishments.

D

Ben Dame is a Vegan Triathlete, Marathon, and Ultradistance Runner. In 2012, he was named one of the national top ten Triathlete in his age group, and represented the United States in the International Triathlete Union Olympic Distance Triathlon World Championship in London in 2021.

Steph Davis is a Vegan Climber who has been a high-profile climber for 25 years. She is one of the most successful climbers globally and the only woman to have free soloed at 5.11 grade. In 2003, she climbed El Capitan which is a 900 meter vertical climb in Yosemite National Park in one day. Only one other woman had ever done it. In 2005, she free-climbed the Salanthe Wall on El Capitan which had never been free-climbed by a woman before. She was also the first woman to climb Torre Egger in Patagonia in one day.

Jermain Colin Defoe is a Vegan former professional Football Player from England who played as a Striker. He began his career with Charlton Athletic, when he joined their youth team at age 14. He then moved to West Ham United at age 16, and rose through the ranks, ultimately playing for the England National Team.

Nimai Delgado is a Vegan Bodybuilder who grew up in Mississippi with Argentinian-immigrant Hare Krishna parents. He has been vegetarian since birth, initially for religious reasons, and has never eaten meat. "Both of my amazing parents are converted Hindus, and I was raised with a strong sense of compassion".

Antoine Jolicoeur Desroches is a Canadian Vegan Triathlete, who won the 2022 Canadaman, and is considered as hardest Ironman triathlon in Canada. He led the swim, which included the Ultraman World

Champion, and led the cycle section, including a 12-minute stop for a train, and completed the marathon leg in 3:42:57 as he challenged for the all-time course record. Antoine finished in 9:40:01! He went so fast through the course that officials were struggled to keep up. Antoine has been vegan for seven years. "I stopped eating meat for animal ethical reasons but my reasons for going vegan were mostly environmental. I watched the Cowspiracy movie and I immediately decided to become vegan."

Nathan Donald Diaz is a Vegan American Professional Mixed Martial Artist who is signed with the Ultimate Fighting Championship. Nathan competed in World Extreme Cagefighting, Strikeforce, and Pancrase.

Yassine Diboun is an American Vegan Ultra Distance Runner of Moroccan and American descent. Since 2007 he won twelve races, ten of which were thirty miles and more. He won and set the course record at the Leona Divide 50k race in 2013 with a time of 4:03:33 and set the course record. He also has 25 top three finishes at 30 miles and above. His results include 100 miles completed in 16 hours 43 minutes and 1 second.

Antonio di Manno is a Vegan Italian Ultradistance Runner who had notable success nationally. He won the six hour Ore di Titina race in 2019, and won first place in the L'Ultimo Sopravvissuto in June 2021. He participated in the Last Survivor race which required competitors to complete a 4.17 mile course every hour until they fail. Antonio won when all the others dropped out after 31 hours. He covered 207 km and qualified for the final in Tennessee, United States of America, against 60 other winners from all over the world.

"It was completely ethical motivation. I have decided and made the change overnight. I run to speak for the animals, and I want to try to talk about veganism as much as possible". Antonio won the 175-mile Milano - San Remo ultramarathon, the longest non-stop Ultramarathon in Europe, which crosses three Italian regions, 54 municipalities, and includes Mount Turchino. He finished in 34 hours 49 minutes. This was three hours and 38 minutes ahead of second place, and only three runners finished in less than 40 hours. Antonio ran with the ear tag of a rescued calf which had died at a sanctuary.

Novak Djokovic is a Serbian Vegan Professional Tennis Player ranked World Number One by the Association of Tennis Professionals as of March 21, 2022. He was ranked World Number One for a record total of 363 weeks and finished as the year-end Number One seven times.

Alina Drozdov is an Israeli Vegan Track Athlete who competes at the national and international levels. She was Israeli National Champion for the 110 m hurdles three times (2017, 2018, and 2019). She is the 5th fastest nationally of all time in this event.

Dusan Dudas is a Vegan Bodybuilder from Slovakia who lives in New Zealand. In 2001, he won 'Mr. New Zealand'. A year later he entered 'Musclemania' in Australia and took second place. In 2007, he won 'Mr. New Zealand Masters'. Two years later he won 'Mr. New Zealand Natural Over 50 Category' at age 54.

Meagan Duhamel is a Vegan from Canada who skated as a single and a pair and is best known for pair skating. She achieved fame when she and her partner, Eric Radford, were the first to perform an amazing side-by-side triple lutz in competition. They are two-time world champions winning both gold medals in both the 2018 Olympics team event and silver medals in the 2014 Olympics team event.

Barny Du Plessis is a Vegan and the winner of 2014 prestigious bodybuilding 'Mr. Universe' competition. He converted fully to a plant-based diet and consumes a hefty 300 grams of plant protein a day. He consumes around 6,000 calories per day during his off-season training.

E

Cleanthony Earlyis a Vegan Professional Basketball Player who was selected with the 34th overall pick in the 2014 NBA draft by the New York Knicks. He played 56 games for the Knicks but in the 2015-2016 season he was robbed at gun point and shot in the right knee. He then signed with Atomeromu SE, a team the top-tier Hungarian league. He was an All-American college player at Wichita State University.

Peter Ebdon is a Vegan and has been a Snooker professional since 1991. He beat former World Champion Steve Davis 10-4 in the 1992 World Championship and was awarded World Professional Billiards and Snooker Association Young Player of the Year award. In 1993 Peter won the Grand Prix, and by 1996 was ranked Number Three internationally.

Maayan Eliasi is an Israeli Vegan Bodybuilder. In 2018 she won first place in the Israeli national NABBA Bikini Division Over 30 category, and won the WNBF Israel in Fit Body Category and Overall Fit Body as well as receiving the WNBF Pro Athlete card.

Cody Elkins is a Vegan Athlete who competed in junior racquetball. In 2013, at age eight, he was the American Junior Champion, and in 2014 he was the California State Champion, as well as many other accomplishments.

Dalila Eshe is a Vegan and a Professional Women's Basketball Player. She has experience in several of the top national leagues and was a Professional Player in Europe for eight years. She plays in the United States Women's National Basketball Association League in the summer, and then plays overseas for the rest of the year.

F

Kendrick James Farris is a Vegan Olympic Weightlifter from the United States. He competed in the 85 kg weight class at the 2008 Summer Olympics and placed 8th. Kendrick also participated in the 2012 Summer Olympics in London where he placed 10th.

Helen Fines is a British Vegan Fell Runner who represents her country. She placed highly nationally, twice finished as the runner up in the British Fell Running Championship, and twice finished second in the English Fell Running Championships.

Claire "Fury" Foreman is an Australian Vegan Muay Thai Martial Artist who won the Victoria WMC Bantamweight title. In November 2015, she fought for the Australian title, and won. She also fought against multiple national champion Sam Brown.

Melanie Fraunschiel is an Austrian Vegan Boxer from Vienna who competes in the 60 kg weight category. When Melanie was 14 years old, she took up full contact karate and competed for ten years. She won numerous medals nationally and internationally.

Mike Fremont is a 96-year-old Vegan Runner who has pushed the boundaries of what is believed to be possible. He retains world records and broke the American road mile record in the 95+ age category with a finish time of 13:55.

G

T J Galiardi is a Vegan and a retired Professional Ice Hockey Player who started playing in the Western Hockey League in 2007. He joined the Calgary Hitmen, and was named the Number Two Rookie in the Western Hockey League with 70 points, leading the league in playoff scoring.

Alister Gardner is a Vegan Trail and Mountain Runner with experience at marathon level and ultramarathon distances. He represented Canada at Mountain Running, as part of a successful team. In 2011 Alister secured a victory in a 50-mile event and cites 2012 as a breakthrough year.

Lisa Gawthorne is a Vegan Duathlon Competitor and an established active multisport athlete. She represents Team Great Britain in Duathlon and competes for European and World honors. In 2017 Lisa qualified for the European Duathlon Championships for her age group.

Sebastian Gergoric is a Slovenian Vegan Triathlete who raced sprint, Olympic, and Ironman distance events. He is best known for his performances at Ironman level. His accomplishments include four full Ironman events completed in under ten hours.

Anthony David Gonzalez is a Vegan and former American football Tight End who played in the National Football League for 17 seasons, primarily with the Kansas City Chiefs.

H

Sir Lewis Carl Davidson Hamilton is a Vegan and a leading British Motorsports Racing Driver. He currently competes in Formula One for Mercedes. He was a six-time World Champion by 2020, the second most of all time, with 88 individual race victories. He previously drove for McLauren from 2007 to 2012. His career total points score was 3,563 as of August 2020 and is considered one of the all-time great Race Drivers.

Damian Hall is a Vegan Ultramarathon Runner who ran his first half marathon at age 35. Attributing it to a midlife crisis, Damian spent the next years reaching astonishing heights in the sport. By 2021, he had seven records and many Fastest Known Times.

Andreas Hanni is a Vegan Ice Hockey Defenseman from Switzerland. He started playing ice hockey in the Swiss National League at age 17, and soon became established player. In 2002, he joined Schlittschuh Club Bern, an ice hockey team based in Bern, Switzerland. They play in the National League, the top tier of the Swiss hockey league system, and with them, he won a National Title.

Adam Hansen is an Australian Vegan Veteran Cyclist who participates in the top cycling events worldwide. In 2003, he competed in two tours and one classic, and by 2019 he had completed 28 grand tours and 12 classics.

David Deron Haye is a British Vegan and former Professional Boxer who competed between 2002 and 2018. He held multiple world championships in two weight classes and was the first British boxer to reach the finals of the World Amateur Boxing Championships. He won a silver medal in 2001.

Craig Health is a Vegan Champion Figure Skater and Choreographer known for his positive attitude and high energy routines. Craig turned professional in 1993 and achieved many notable career highlights. In 1990 he visited England and won Skate Electric, and in 1991, he won the US National Championships.

Ruth Heidrich is a Vegan Runner who has maintained an astonishing level of fitness.

Ruth embraced a vegan lifestyle in 1982, at age 47, in response to a diagnosis of aggressive breast cancer. She not only survived, but won over 900 medals for running all distances, up to and including ironman triathlon.

Julia Hubbard is a Vegan who was a member of the British Bobsled team from 2006 to 2010. She competed internationally in Bobsleigh, Bodybuilding, Fitness and Sprinting. Julia was born with a heart condition which was not diagnosed until 2009. She competed in the European and World Cups until a bobsled crash broke her back. Then, Julia started bodybuilding, and by the end of July 2017 she competed over fifty times, taking first place in one or more categories in an amazing twenty- seven of those competitions including national and international competitions and world titles. Julia also competed in sprinting after the crash, and was World Masters Champion at 200 meters, in addition to wining several British indoor titles. Julia is a qualified Vegan Nutritionist and has a Degree in

Physiology and Sports Science, Nutrition diploma and Personal Training qualifications. Julia currently works in a job she loves as an online personal trainer.

I

Mika Ireste is a Vegan and leading player in the brutal and sometimes dangerous contact sport of Roller Derby. She plays in Wales for Swansea City under the name 'Little Myy'. She also plays for Team Wales as 'Ireste'. Roller Derby involves two teams skating in the same direction around a track.

Kyrie Andrew Irving is a Vegan and a United States Professional Basketball Player for the Brooklyn Nets of the National Basketball Association. He was named the Rookie of the Year after being selected by the Cleveland Cavaliers with the first overall pick in the 2011 NBA draft.

Vlad Ixel is a Vegan Runner who competes in the extreme sport of ultradistance marathon running. He started running in

2012 and turned vegan shortly afterward. He ran the 75km KEP ultramarathon in Perth, Australia, and won by over 5 minutes.

J

Johanna Jahnke is a Vegan Rugby Player and Cyclist who made an impact in two major sports since becoming vegan. She twice captained her Rugby Union Club Team F C St. Pauli in Hamburg, Germany and helped FC St Pauli Hamburg to 10 National Championships. She has also established herself as a world class fixed gear cyclist

Emily Jans is a retired Vegan Professional Kickboxer who won the 2012 Australian Amateur Boxing title in the Elite Women's 64kg division. According to Emily, "I think I'm proof that being vegan is great for training. I not only have physically demanding employment and hobbies, but most of the time I ride my push bike as transportation".

Bryant Jennings is a Vegan Heavyweight Boxer with international records, including two title challenges, two world professional heavyweight title challenges, World Champion Klitschko full distance, and has won World Class Boxer for many years.

Hege Jenssen is a Norwegian Vegan Pro-Level Kettlebell Competitor who has competed nationally and in international competitions. She excels in Snatch, and on her debut in the professional class she took 5th place at the World Championships.

Catherine (Cat) Johnson is a Vegan Cyclocross Champion who has been vegan since1998 at age 22. She expresses her reason for being a Vegan: "I did not want to cause suffering to animals. I knew that animals often lived under horrible conditions on factory farms, and that they do not have voices to scream and yell to their abusers, leaving them totally defenseless."

Sofia Jokl is a Vegan Competitor in Japanese Ju-Jitsu in the Duo-System at European and World level. The Duo system involves pairs of competitors demonstrating self-defense against attacks randomly called by a referee.

Antoine Jolicoeur is a Canadian Vegan Multisport Athlete specializing in Triathlon. His strongest distance is the Half Ironman. This is a 1.9 km (1.2 mile) swim, 90 km (56 mile) cycle and a 21.1 km (13.1 mile) run.

Kuntal Joisher is a Vegan Mountaineer from India who has pushed the boundaries of his sport with some amazing climbs. In October 2014, he climbed Mount Manaslu, which is 8,163 meters high, and the eighth highest mountain in the world. In May 2016 he climbed the south side of Mount Everest.

Ellen Jaffe Jones is a Vegan and a United States Health and Fitness Journalist, Author, Speaker, and Athlete. She is the author of "Eat Vegan on $4 a Day--A Game Plan for the Budget Conscious Cook", published in 2011, and "The Kitchen Divided-Vegan Recipes for the Semi-Vegan Household", published in 2013. Ellen is also a Vegan Senior Runner who competes in distances from 100 meters to endurance distances. She was successful in the 2012 Florida State Senior Games which made her eligible to compete in the Senior National Competition in four separate events.

According to Ellen, "After a 5K I ran in Florida in 2011, I was on the podium holding a trophy and wearing a bright neon yellow shirt with the cover of my book "Eat Vegan on $4 a Day" on it," she recalls. "This guy tells me, "You can't run on a vegan diet, and you certainly can't race on a vegan diet." At that point, I had been running for 30 years and answered, "Let's have that conversation." Also, "There's a perception that vegans are weak and all they eat is spinach and broccoli with no variety. Nothing could be farther from the truth!"

Deandre Jordan is a Vegan Basketball Player in the National Basketball Association with the Los Angeles Lakers, and was the 35th pick of the 2008 draft at age 20. He averages 10.6 rebounds per game, is a three time all NBA team member, a two time All-Defensive Team member, and NBA All-Star in 2017. He has the record for best field goal percentage, 67.39%, and is also known as a strong post-defender, with a career average of 1.6 blocks per game. His endurance is amazing. At one point he had played 360 games without resting.

Scott Gordon Jurek is a Vegan American Ultramarathon Runner from Colorado. Ultramarathon distances are beyond the standard marathon of 26.2 miles (42km). Throughout his running career, Scott was one of the most dominant ultramarathon runners in the world. He led the sport with some amazing performances including multiple wins and course records. He won the Hardrock Hundred, the Badwater Ultramarathon, the Spartathlon, and the Western States 100 Mile Endurance Run. Scott is also an Author and Public Speaker.

K

Colin Rand Kaepernick is a Vegan former Football Quarterback who played six seasons for the San Francisco 49ers in the

National Football League. He is currently an American civil rights activist.

Fia Kamlund from Sweden is a Vegan Powerlifter who built up amazing strength and much success. She is in the 84kg category in both raw and equipped and has achieved 430 kg raw and 512.5 kg equipped totals in competition.

Dawid Kawka is a Vegan Polish Powerlifter who made his mark on the 2020 National Championships with some enormous lifts. He competed at 74kg with the International Powerlifting Federation and squatted more than three times his bodyweight at the Championships, breaking the national Polish record with a 250 kg squat.

Niki Kelly is a Vegan Professional Snowboarder from rural Canada. She pursues her passions of nature, photography, and snowboarding, lives in her van with her partner Mitch and dog Nelson. Niki explores on her sled and on foot, and she competes!

Tammy Fry Kelly is a Vegan from South Africa who is well known for her business activities and her achievements in sports. She is a Karate 5th Dan Black Belt, has competed nationally and internationally for over twenty years, and was part of the South African Senior National Karate team for ten years.

Hollie Kempton is a Vegan Powerlifter who is incredibly strong and has achieved some amazing lifts. She competes in the 48 kg category and has squatted 105 kg and benched 60 kg. Her deadlift is over three times her bodyweight at 155 kg. Unsurprisingly, Hollie feels that her deadlift is her greatest achievement.

Joel Kirkilis is an Australian Vegan Bodybuilder who became the Victoria (Australia) Bodybuilding Champion in 2009. In 2010, he entered the International Natural Bodybuilding Association, Melbourne Open, and the Victoria Class 2 Competition. He finished second in each and has since been working on technique and coaching other athletes.

Laura Kline is a Vegan Multisport Athlete from Pasadena, California. She is best known for her success in the Duathlon, an endurance event which starts with a run, changes to cycling, then returns to running. She participated in hockey, softball, basketball and boxing while in high school and college. At age 26, she started competing in the demanding sports of Duathlon and Triathlon. She qualified for the World Championships at her debut in 2004.

L

Sahyuri (Sahy) Lalime is a Belgium Vegan Powerlifter with Japanese American ancestry. She competed nationally and internationally and in 2018 and 2019 she won Best Overall Female Powerlifter in the Belgian Nationals and competed at the IPF World and European Championships

Andrew Lally is an American Vegan Professional Auto Racing Driver who competes full-time in the Weather Tech Sports Car Championship. He drives the Audi R8 for Magnus Racing and competes part-time in the NASCAR Cup Series, driving the No. 78 Ford Mustang for Live Fast Motorsports. Andy won the Rolex 24 hour event at the Daytona International Speedway in 2001, 2009, 2011, 2012, and 2016 and holds the record for the most podium finishes in this race since the Grand Am era started in 2000!

Kara Lang is a Vegan and former member of the Canadian Women's Football Team who played successfully at the club and national levels. Kara started playing at the highest levels at a very young age, and at age 15 years and 132 days, she took the world record for the youngest player to score a full international goal – a record which still stands today. Two days later she set the record for the youngest Canadian senior women's appearance.

Georges Edy Laraque is a Vegan and a Canadian Sports Commentator for TVA Sports, a Politician, and former Ice Hockey

Player. He is 6'3" tall and weighs 116 kg, making him a formidable opponent on the ice. Georges played in the lower leagues before joining Edmonton in the Canadian National Hockey League in the 1997-98 season. He gained a reputation as an aggressive player and was unanimously named "Best Fighter" by Hockey News in 2003. He retired from hockey in 2010 after the Montreal Canadiens bought out his contract. He recently became Executive Director of the fledgling Canadian Hockey League Players' Association.

Juanjo Larrotcha is a Vegan Ultra Distance Runner from Spain who excels in incredibly demanding races, although he is currently well into middle age. He has taken an incredible 17 overall victories in trail and ultra-trail races, including a win in the 2017 Nepalese Annapurna 100 km race, which is over 5500 meters in height.

Massimo Leopardi is a Vegan Educator and Diver from Italy who started training in Diving at age 49. He strived to promote vegan ideals in Italy through education and by personal example as an internationally competitive athlete.

Frederick Carlton Lewis is an American Vegan and former track and field athlete who won nine Olympic gold medals, one Olympic silver medal, and 10 World Championships medals, including eight gold. His career spanned from 1979 to 1996, when he won an Olympic event.

Harvey Sweetland Lewis is a Vegan American ultrarunner who won the Badwater Ultramarathon twice. This race is considered one of the toughest footraces in the world. The 135-mile race features extreme temperatures and massive height gain and losses. Harvey represented Team USA at the International Association of Ultrarunners 24 Hour World Championship in 2012, 2013, 2014, and 2017!

Jack Linquist is a Vegan Professional Track Racing Cyclist who won his first race in 2007. He was a 26-year-old cycle messenger when he won the Puma Velocity race in New York City. The win entitled him to a place in international competitions, and he soon joined the United States team.

SuzAnne Llano is a Vegan Natural Bodybuilder. She has always been athletic. Initially she enjoyed soccer and ballet. SuzAnne started serious Bodybuilding training in 2009. Currently she has entered over twenty competitions and has taken wins and podium places. Additionally, she won the elite accolade of Pro Card holder in three federations: National Gym Association, American Natural Bodybuilding Foundation, and Natural Fit Foundation.

M

Auryn MacMillan is an Australian Vegan Professional Basketballer in the National League. He plays in Australia, Germany, and the UK. He is a power forward known for his high energy.

Dean Mahar is a Vegan Mountain Climber who reached the top of Everest, one of the greatest achievements in mountaineering, on his fourth trip to the Himalayas. He previously climbed Himlung Himal

(7,126m), Imja Tse (Island Peak, 6,189 m) and Lobuche East (6,119m). He also trekked the 3 Passes, Annapurna Circuit and Annapurna Base Camp. He uses all vegan gear and clothing.

Jehina Malik is a Vegan Bodybuilder who has competed since she was 19 years old and is recognized as an accomplished competitor with an impressive physique. She won first place in women's physique and first place over all at the NPC Eastern USA Bodybuilding Championship in 2013, and was in her first international show, Team Universe, in 2014.

Bill McCarthy is an American Vegan Powerlifter who competes at the national level, and in international competitions including the Arnold Sports festival. His personal best lifts (raw) are 501 lb (227.5 kg) bench press, 750 lbs (340 kg) squat and 622 lb (282.5 kg) deadlift.

David Meyer is a Vegan who has competes in the Martial Art of Brazilian Jiu Jitsu. Over the years, David won numerous international titles. He is recognized as a pioneer of the sport and one of the first non-Brazilians to achieve a black belt.

Denis Mikhaylove is a Vegan Ultradistance Runner. He was born in Russia and moved to New York in 2006. He moved to develop a career in finance but by 2010 he gave it up to pursue one in health and fitness. He became an Ultradistance Runner, and in 2011 he took four top five finishes.

Heather Mills is a Vegan Downhill Skier also known for her work as an entrepreneur and a campaigner. She has campaigned on the issue of landmines for fourteen years and raised funds and awareness.

Morgan Mitchell is a Vegan Australian athlete who ran the 800m in the 2021 Tokyo Summer Olympics and was a semi-finalist in the 400m at the 2016 Rio Summer Olympics. She says, "Going vegan has helped a lot. I recover a lot quicker than I used to. It's easier to keep my weight down, and I haven't been sick at all."

Naomi Mitchell is a Vegan Runner who races nationally from over 5k to marathon distance. She had 2020 half marathon personal best of 1:15:19. and has since improved on it.

Elena Congost Mohedano is a Vegan, Teacher, and a T12/B2 track and field athlete. Elena was born with a degenerative vision impairment. She competed at the 2004, 2008, 2012 and 2016 Summer Paralympics, representing Spain. She won the marathon in 2016 and placed second in the 1,500 m in 2012, and is known for her remarkable versatility in long jump, 100 meters, and marathon

Greg Moormann is a Vegan Natural Bodybuilder with numerous wins in the Master categories. He is a Pro card holder with both the National Gym Association and American Natural Bodybuilding Federation which are only awarded after having reached an elite standard.

Derrick Lee Morgan is a Vegan and a former American Football Linebacker who spent his entire nine-year pro career playing for the Tennessee Titans of the National Football League. He was selected 16th overall by the Titans in the 2010 NFL draft after playing college football at Georgia Tech.

Jim Morris is an American Vegan Bodybuilder. In 1966, he entered his first competition and became Mr. New York City. He was 31 years old at the time. The following year, he won his first national title, Mr. East Coast. He won many competitions during his thirty-year career, including Mr. USA, AAU Mr. America, Mr. International, and Mr. Olympia Masters Over 60.

Nigel Morton is a Vegan Powerlifter and Trainer. He has had national success with some amazing lifts. He competed in the Canadian Nationals in 2017 where the 126 kg lifter squatted an enormous 300 kg, benched 195 kg and finished with even more.

Anthony Winston Mullally is a Vegan Rugby League Professional who is also known by the nickname of "Vegan Warrior". He played internationally in the English, Canadian and Irish leagues. He is currently an Ireland International Rugby League Footballer and plays as a Pro for Cornwall Rugby League Football Club (RLFB) in Betfred League One. He previously played for the French Club Carcassonne and the Widnes Vikings in the Championship and the Super League.

Leilani Munter is a Vegan American Racing Driver and Environmental Activist. She started racing in 2001 at age 25. Two years later she started in the NASCAR weekly racing series. In 2004, she made her first Speedway Start and qualified in fourth place setting a Women's Record.

N

Pat Neshek is a Vegan Baseball Player whose skills were noticed at an early age and he was selected for the All-State team. He took the school record for strike outs in a single game, in a season, and in a career. At age 18 he had the opportunity to play in the Major Leagues.

Cam Newton is a Vegan who plays Football in the United States National Football League as a Quarterback for the New England Patriots. He became an established player with some fantastic NFL records including seven NFL all-time records, 21 NFL firsts, and NFL record for quarterback rushing touchdowns.

Harri Nieminem is a Vegan and former World Champion Thai Boxer. Harri travelled to Thailand to win the 1997 Thai Boxing title. He beat the US Champion in the Semi and the Thai Champion in the Final. Harri was 22 when he started eating vegan in 1994 and never regretted it or turned back.

O

Fiona Oakes is a Vegan British Distance Runner who has made great achievements in running. She holds four world records for marathon running. In 2013, she won both the Antarctic Ice Marathon and the North Pole Marathon. She runs despite losing a kneecap due to a tumor when she was 17. Her training competes with other demands on her time and energy including being on call in her work as a Retained Firefighter. Fiona has been vegan since she was 6 years old.

Lawrence Okolie is a British Vegan Boxer who has risen through the ranks to become a world-recognized force in Professional boxing. By 2018, he held the Commonwealth cruiserweight title. In 2019, he won the British and European titles in the same category, and in 2020, he won the World title.

Jay Oliveira is a Vegan who made a rapid impact on the martial art of Brazilian Jiu Jitsu. In 2016 he fought in the Brown Belt Masters Division and entered five international tournaments sanctioned by the lead federation IBJFF. He took Gold in all 5 tournaments.

Nienke Overved is a Vegan Athlete in the demanding sport of CrossFit. She competes internationally and was crowned "Fittest woman in the Netherlands 2020" after winning the CrossFit Open. She qualified for CrossFit Games World Championships on Team Vondelgym in 2019.

P

Micky Papa is a Vegan Canadian Skateboarder who competed in the Summer Olympics in 2021 and was one of my personal favorites. He currently resides in California.

Chris Paul is a Vegan Point Guard Basketball Player on the United States National Basketball Association Phoenix Suns and was named NBA Rookie of the Year. He also won the NBA All-Star Game Most Valuable Player Award and has won two Olympic gold medals.

Yolanda Presswood is a Vegan Powerlifter who originally competed in the Bikini and Fitness categories of Bodybuilding.

Yolanda started competing in Crossfit in November 2014, then moved to Powerlifting in October 2016.

Glenda Presutti is a Vegan Powerlifter who was originally a Registered Nurse. She embraced Powerlifting relatively late, at age 62 in 2018. Glenda took the sport by storm and rapidly emerged as a force recognized nationally and internationally and overcame numerous injuries.

Spencer Pumpelly is a Vegan who is considered one of the most successful drivers in North American Race Car Driving. He competed at the top level for over twenty years. Spencer scored wins in the American Le Mans series and the Grand-Am Rolex Series.

Joni Purmonen is a Strongman who has been a Vegan since 1991. In 2000, he started competing in 105 kg weight category events. Since then, he developed an impressive level of strength, with personal bests of 150kg for bench press, 230kg for squat and a deadlift of 262.5kg.

R

Pat Reeves is a Vegan Powerlifter who competes at 42.9kg bodyweight. Pat's personal bests include: 90kg Squat, 55kg Bench Press (a British record) and 130kg Deadlift. Pat was diagnosed with a serious genetic cancer in 1977 when she was 32 years old. The devastating news led her to adopt a wholefood plant-based Vegan diet. As a result, she has made an excellent recovery. and the 'terminal' cancer went into remission.

Weia Reinboud is a Vegan Track and Field Athlete and a veteran athletics multiple world record holder. She started competing in Masters Athletics in 1995 at age 45, after decades of not training. By 1999, she was competing in Gateshead, UK, where she came in second to an athlete who set a world record for the women's age 45 age category.

Kane Richardson is a Vegan from Australia who is making his mark on Cricket at home and abroad. He is sought after in the exciting short forms of the game and became famous in his native country. Kane is a right-arm medium-fast bowler who represented his nation in 25 One Day Internationals and 26 Twenty 20 matches.

Amanda Riester is a Vegan Boxer whose two Grandfathers and Father boxed professionally. Inspired by them, Amanda entered the Chicago Golden Gloves amateur competition at age 16. At age 17, Amanda boxed at the national level. At age18, she was rated number two in the United States.

Neil Robertson is a Vegan World Champion Snooker Player from Austria who topped the international snooker rankings. Neil is one of the best known and highest achieving players in snooker. He is a former world champion and former world number one._Neil was born in Liverpool close to the Everton Football Club, which he supported, and grew up in Merseyside, North West England, an area known for Soccer enthusiasm. Despite his school concentration on Rugby, Neil always wanted to play Professional Football. Neil was most proud of his ethical choices, "I am a former professional footballer from the UK, and I was also the very first known ethical VEGAN professional footballer anywhere in the world!"

Rich Roll is an American Vegan Ultra-Endurance Athlete. Rich became a world recognized athlete at age 40 when he realized his health was being threatened by his lifestyle, use of alcohol and drugs, poor diet, and inactivity. When he was unable to climb stairs, he decided to adopt a whole food plant-based vegan diet and lifestyle and began athletic training. He not only accomplished his goal of restoring his health but became an outstanding athlete, as well. He is currently a full-time wellness and plant-based nutrition advocate, popular public speaker, husband, father of four and an inspiration to people worldwide as a transformative example of courageous and healthy living.

Ariel Rosenfeld is an Israeli Vegan Ultramarathon Runner who won Sovev

Emek, the most prominent Israeli ultramarathon four times in recent years, won the 61 km race in 2011, 2012 and 2014, and competed outside of Israel.

Maureen (Mo) Bruno-Roy is a Vegan Cyclocross Cyclist who has competed at the elite level for many years. She began racing at that level in 2004 and in 2005 and finished third in the Elite Women's National Championships. Mo also became National Champion in the 30-34 age category.

John Rush is an American Vegan Footballer who plays fullback for the Winnipeg Blue Bombers in the Canadian Football League (CFL). John played successfully in college from 2011 to 2015, and then went on to play for the Blue Bombers in 2015.

S

Melody Schoenfeld is a Vegan and successful Powerlifter. She has records at State and National level. The petite American has shown enormous strength in kettlebell, and old time strongman challenges including bar bending. Melody broke California State Records for all three lifts, bench press, squat, and deadlift.

Shelli Beecher-Seitzler is a Vegan Natural Bodybuilder who made an impressive impact on the sport. She trained six days a week and after five months entered the 2018 INBF NW Royal Natural Bodybuilding Championship.

Kevin Selker is a Vegan American Track Cyclist who has been competing in sprint events since 2005 when he was 20 years old. He recorded placings at the National Collegiate level. In December 2006, Kevin was a National Senior Champion and selected for the United States National Squad.

Madi Serpico is a Vegan Triathlete who at age 21, in 2014, had already competed nationally and internationally. Her results include 15th in the International Edmonton World Cup in 2012; 13th in the 2012 Pan

American Cup (Magog); and 10th in the Canadian National Championships.

Alberto Pelaez Serrano is a Vegan and an experienced Ultramarathon Runner. He won twelve Ultramarathons and Marathons, including the high profile 'Ultramarathon of Lanzarote' three times. He has the speed record for ascending and descending the Toubkal Mountain in Morocco which is 167 meters of height.

Alex Shelley is a Vegan who won the World Champion Fitness title with the World Fitness Federation. He became a vegan in response to the cruelty of the animal food industries. His motivation was "ethical, ecological, spiritual and healthy reasons, in that order."

Timothy Shieff is a Vegan and an English Free Runner who won the Barclaycard World Free Run Championship in 2009. He participated on MTV's Ultimate Parkour Challenge and competed on American Ninja Warrior and Ninja Warrior UK.

Peter Matthew Siddle is an Australian Vegan Cricketer who specializes in right-arm fast-medium bowler and bowled for Essex and Victoria. Peter is a right arm fast bowler who started playing regularly for Victoria in the 2006-7 season, at age 22. By 2008 he already caught the attention of the national selectors and went on a Cricketer tour of India with Australia. He currently plays for Tasmania in first-class and List A cricket and plays for the Adelaide Strikers in the Big Bash League.

Christopher Lloyd Smalling is a Vegan English Soccer Player who played Center Back for the world-famous Manchester United in the English Premier League. He was also picked for the English National Team and now plays as a Center-Back for Serie A Club Roma. Chris signed for United in 2010 at age 21 and helped the club to achieve the FA Cup in 2016, Europe League title in 2016-7, and an English league title also in 2016-7. Playing defense had not stopped Chris from scoring 12 goals. At the end 2018-9 season, Chris had made

206 appearances. During his youth played for the Millwall Academy before joining non-League Club Maidstone United and ultimately Serie A Club Roma.

David Smith is a successful Vegan Para Rower and Cyclist who won Gold medals at the international level and overcame enormous setbacks. David was born with a club foot, and Doctors considered full amputation of his foot at birth. David underwent repeated medical interventions to break and reset his foot. He recovered to extremely high levels of fitness which he attributes to determination and high standards of plant-based nutrition. In 2009, he took up para rowing and joined a coxed four team in the disability LTAM ix4 category. The Team won Gold at the 2009 World Rowing Championships. David participated in the same event at the World Championships and won Gold in 3 minutes 27.10 seconds, a win by almost 5 seconds.

James Southwood is a Vegan Instructor and Champion Fighter in Savate, a dynamic sport that combines movements from English boxing and French kicking. He is a multiple Great British Champion, 2008 World Bronze Medalist, European Silver Medalist twice, 2016 World Vice-Champion, and 2014 World Champion.

Nick Squires is an accomplished Vegan Powerlifter who competes in the raw divisions in California and internationally. He won in his category and 2nd overall in IPL World Championships in 2019. He broke the California Deadlift record (295kg) and won the 2019 California State Championships with a 255 kg squat at 110 kg bodyweight and Drug Tested Competitor and he has taken overall first place in the LA Open.

Ana Stefulj is a Vegan Runner from Croatia who made a big impact in distance running at national and international levels. Ana took her first medal at the National Championship in 2019 in the 1:20 half marathon.

Sarah Stewart is a Vegan Australian 3.0-point Wheelchair Basketball Player. She started playing in 2001, and in two years made the national team. In 2004, her team won the Silver Medal in the Summer Paralympics in Athens, and in 2008 her team won the Bronze medal in the Paralympics in Beijing, and in 2012 her team won a Silver medal in the Summer Paralympics in London.

Ryan Stills is a world class Vegan Powerlifter who has competed at the highest level against the strongest opponents. He competed in raw divisions with IPF and USAPL in the 120 kilogram category, and this includes four category wins at the IPF Masters World Championships.

Damian Stoy has been a prominent Vegan Ultradistance Runner since 2006, with numerous podium finishes and race victories. He won Grand Teton 50 miler in 2006, then recorded four second places before taking three wins in 2010, two of which were records on 50-mile courses.

Melissa Sundermann is a Vegan Endurance Racer who competes in Cycling, Running and Multisport Events. She covers epic distances at elite times and was the first Amateur woman at the REV3 Ironman Triathlon. She finished with a personal best of 10:57:20, crossing the line with her husband and children.

T

Or Tal is an Israeli Swimmer who has been a Vegan since age nine. He competed in the Emek Hefer Championships where he was one of 800 swimmers from 44 teams across Israel. He took Gold in the 100 meters freestyle, 200 meters freestyle, and the 400 meters freestyle. He then entered the 800 meters and took Bronze. Or was also part of the mixed relay team and took Gold in the 4 x 50 meters. The men's title for outstanding male swimmer was awarded to Or. He trains with, and competes for, the Hapoel Bat – Yam Team.

Diana Taurasi is a Vegan National and International Women's Basketball Player.

Diana has achieved amazing things during her career. At age 37, Diana played for the Phoenix Mercury in the Women's National Basketball Association in the United States of America (2020). She won three Championships, one WNBA Most Valuable Player Award, two WNBA Finals MVP Awards and four Olympic medals.

Ed Templeton is a Vegan Skater from California. Ed started skating in the 1980's and in 1988, when he was 16 years old, he was sponsored. He turned Professional in 1990 and was featured on the front covers of the skateboard magazines 'Trans World Skateboarding' and 'Thrasher'.

Hannah Teter is a Vegan and a Champion American Snowboarder. She won a gold medal in the halfpipe in the 2006 Winter Olympics in Torino, Italy and a silver medal in the 2010 Winter Olympics in Vancouver, Canada.

Derek Tresize is a Professional Bodybuilder and has been a Vegan since 2007. He has a Bachelor of Science in

Biology, is a Personal Trainer through the American Council on Exercise and has a Certificate in Plant-Based Nutrition through Cornell University.

Abel Nazario Trujillo is an American Vegan Mixed Martial Artist who competes in the Lightweight division of the Ultimate Fighting Championship.

V

Christine Vardaros is a Vegan Cyclist who won the 2004 Santa Cruz Classic Criterium. In 2001, she made the US National Team and competed in the Cyclo-Cross World Championships. She took 9th place in the Netherlands Heerlen World Cup, and 8th place in the Wetzikon World Cup.

David Verburg is a Vegan United States Track and Field athlete who competes internationally. He had most success over 400 meters individually, and in the 4 x 400 meters relay. He won a Gold medal with the US team in the 2016 Rio Olympics and competed in the 2013 and 2015 World

Championships and in the 2014 Indoor World Championship.

Andreas Vojta is a Vegan Austrian Distance Runner and Track Athlete who became the leading national track runner and a successful international competitor. Andreas competed in the 1,500 meters competition at the 2012 Summer Olympics. Andreas' personal bests are 3:36 for the 1500 meters, 13.38 for 5,000 meters, and 28:33 for the 10,000 meters.

Alexey Ivanovich Voyevoda is a Vegan and an outstanding Russian bobsledder, professional arm wrestler and politician.

W

Hulda B. Waage is a Vegan Powerlifter from Iceland who established herself as a leading Powerlifter. She has competed in raw and equipped powerlifting and holds several national records.

Vivian Kong Man Wai is a Vegan Hong Kongese left-handed épée fencer, 2018 individual Asian champion, and 2016 &

2020 Olympian. Kong became the first Hong Kongese fencer to win a World Cup title when she won the FIE Women's Épée World Cup in Havana, Cuba in January 2019. She thought about becoming vegan for several years, but it took a serious injury to convince her to adopt a plant-based diet. She says it played a big part in her recovery, and her return to the top of the sport. According to Vivian, she has all the protein she needs and feels much stronger after becoming a vegan.

Torre Washington is a Professional Bodybuilder, NASM Certified Coach, Sprinter, and Animal Lover. Torre studied the physiques of Arnold Schwarzenegger and others and began sculpting his body with a dumbbell and a bench. He has a degree in engineering, but his passion for sculpting physiques led him to learn about bodybuilding and begin competing. He is now one of the fitness experts and shares his gift with the world.

Dustin Joseph Watten is a Vegan and an American Volleyball Player. He is a member of the United States Men's National Volleyball Team, and a Gold Medalist at the 2015 World Cup. In addition to playing for his own nation, he played in the Brazilian National Leagues and LUK Lublin, Poland.

Shea West is a Vegan BMX Bicycle Moto Cross Rider from Kansas. He started riding competitively in childhood and won several State Championship titles and ultimately placed fourth in the 1994 World championships. He was also part of the team that won a National Team Title in 1993.

Griff Whalen is an American Vegan Football Player in the National Football League who played with the San Diego Colts, the Baltimore Ravens, the Indianapolis Colts, the Miami Dolphins and Stanford University. He is currently signed with the Oakland Raiders.

James Brett Wilks is a Vegan and an English Film Producer, a Vegan Activist, a

Combative Expert and Instructor, and Former Professional Mixed Martial Artist. He competed for the UFC, King of the Cage in 2003 until 2012, and was the winner of Spike TV's The Ultimate Fighter: United States vs. United Kingdom

Venus Ebony Starr Williams is a Vegan American Professional Tennis Player, and a former world No. 1 in singles and doubles. Venus won seven Grand Slam singles titles, five at Wimbledon, and two at the US Open, and is widely regarded as one of the all-time tennis greats.

Z

Adam Zampa is a Vegan Spin Bowler from Australia and one of the most respected spin bowlers of his generation. He represented South Australia and the Australian National team and played with the Melbourne Stars and Sydney Thunder. Adam also had success in the 20 Twenty format in some of the most competitive competitions on the globe.

Michael Zigomanis is a Vegan and former Canadian Professional Ice Hockey Centre who was drafted twice. In the 1999 NHL Entry Draft he was selected 64th overall by the Buffalo Sabres. He was not signed, but re-entered for the 2001 NHL Entry Draft, and was selected by the Carolina Hurricanes 46th overall. He played regularly as a Forward for the Toronto Maple Leafs and Toronto Marlies.

Anastasia Zinchenko is a Vegan Athlete who holds a PhD in Biochemistry from Cambridge University. She became a vegan to improve her performance. "However, the more information I gained about the negative impact of factory farming, the more my decision of living a vegan lifestyle became motivated by morality. I don't want to support something, and contribute to something, I consider as being wrong or unnecessary."

Anastasia competes in the 63kg and 72 kg weight classes, and has taken regional UK titles, and national placings. She competed in Israel, weighing in at 68.9 kg and competed in the 75 kg category. She started with a 130 kg squat, which was a personal best. Her 82.5 kg bench was another personal best and she added a PB 150 kg deadlift. In 2014, she won the BDFPA All Midlands Championships, 72 kg weight class, and took second in the 2014 British Universities Powerlifting Championship, 63 kg class. She won the Anglian Open Powerlifting Championship 72 kg weight class in 2015 and took place 6th at the GBPF British Classic Powerlifting Championships in the 63 kg class. Anastasia took 2nd at the 2015 GBPF East Midlands Senior Powerlifting Championship (72 kg) and the 2016 National British Classic Bench Press Championships (72 kg). She placed 3rd at the 2017 USPA Naturally Fit Games (67.5 kg), as well as other impressive wins.

Chapter 9

Protein:
Winners and Losers

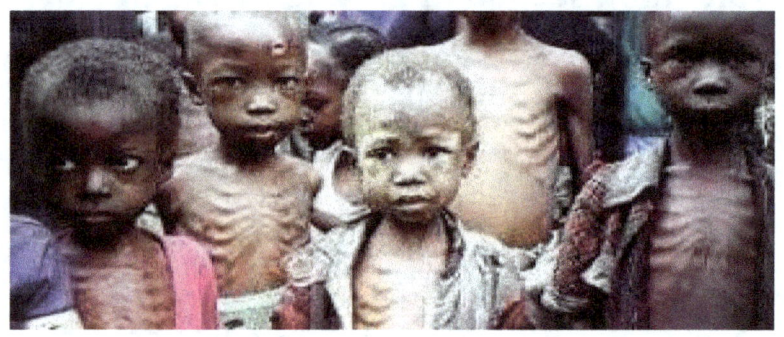

Did you know there are winners and losers in the "Protein" game?

The unfortunate losers are those individuals who were conditioned to believe that they need secondary protein for their health, when in fact, just the opposite is true. The meat and dairy based diet is linked to heart disease, diabetes, some cancers, antibiotic resistance, toxicity, and most require copious amounts of medication - which has copious amounts of side effects, including financial costs.

Other losers include those unfortunate individuals who have no rights, their children and their secretions, which are considered by some to be "protein", and most importantly, those individuals suffering from hunger and starvation because grain that could have been used to save their lives was fed to incarcerated individuals in animal agriculture.

The winners, however, are just the opposite. By contemporary standards, they are doing quite well. They receive obscene amounts of money to do with as they wish and indulge themselves in all kinds of luxuries. Where does this money come from? You – of course! Today in the United States, the cost of the meat and dairy based diet is kept artificially low by the use of United States tax-payer dollars. This is done in the form of "Subsidies". It occurs in other parts of the world as well.

Billions of dollars in subsidies and compensation are provided to animal agriculture every year by Politicians who prefer not to address the impact of animal agriculture on human health, the environment, or defenseless innocent animals. These Lawmakers continue to provide taxpayer funded subsidies to the unhealthy and environmentally destructive meat and dairy industry in return for contributions to their political campaigns.

The U.S. government spends up to approximately $40 billion each year subsidizing agriculture mostly for the meat and dairy industries. Less than one percent of that is allocated to assist the production of fruits and vegetables. Most agricultural subsidies go to farmers of livestock – the large scale meat and dairy producers, also known as "factory farms".

In addition, corn and soy inputs used to feed incarcerated animals are heavily subsidized with US taxpayer dollars. These crops are used in the production of meat and processed food by some of the world's largest and richest meat and dairy corporations. Multibillion- dollar corporations hardly need the tax dollars of hard-working, often struggling, individual Americans to supplement their profits, but they get it!

The farm subsidy programs offer financial protection against adverse fluctuations in revenues and production, pays for insurance, marketing, export sales expenses, research and development, and protects against 'economic loss' resulting from neglect and abuse of the sentient beings they are exploiting. Shoppers pay artificially lower prices for meat and dairy at the checkout counter, while behind the scenes, their tax dollars fund major meat operations and their extensive advertising. Meanwhile, meat and dairy producers accrue yearly retail sales of roughly 250 billion dollars!

"Meatonomics" by David Simon explains that consumers pay an estimated $2 of invisible costs for every $1 of product the meat and dairy industry sells though their tax payer funded subsidies. By these calculations, a $4 Big Mac actually costs society $12.

The other winners in this game are the lucky politicians who control the subsidies. In return for their generosity with OPM (Other Peoples' Money), they are rewarded by the beneficiaries of these subsidy windfalls with generous political campaign contributions. They keep their prestigious jobs, stay in power, and continue to unethically squander tax dollars while amassing private fortunes of their own resulting from political payoffs from the meat and dairy industry.

According to David Robinson Simon in "Meatonomics", "One study found that in connection with Federal subsidy legislation, a $1 industry donation typically yields a $2,000 return in the form of subsidy payments. It's a rate of return so high, most businesspeople would say its impossible. So, is it any wonder that the animal food industry spends more than $100 million yearly paying lobbyists and making strategic donations? A look at the industry's dozens of legislative victories in recent decades shows that this spending is yielding more than robust subsidies. Its also paying back animal food producers in the form of valuable laws that protect and insulate industry players and lower their costs of doing business."

Losers include the environment - land, air, water, and hungry people. Land: forests are cut down to provide grazing, causing desertification. Air: methane and other gases hold heat and cause pollution. Water: toxic waste from animal agriculture enters aquifers and pollutes drinking water. Secondary protein insatiability is the biggest driver of climate disruption involving rising temperatures, rising waters globally, and severe weather incidents such as hurricanes and tornados.

Losers in the protein game are not limited to US borders. A recent September 2021 report by the United Nations Food and Agriculture Organization (UN FAO), states that agricultural subsidies in economically advanced countries, such as the United States, artificially depress international market prices forcing poorer nations to import food. Farmers in the developing world are forced to leave the market because they can't afford to grow local crops or feed their families. UN FAO reports that eliminating agricultural subsidies in the U.S. alone would lift millions of people out of poverty worldwide.

U.S. Government political subsidies are not limited to meat and dairy, they include other individuals capable of feeling pain and suffering – fish and 'sea food'.

If humans continue fishing at the current levels, research published in "Science" predicts the collapse of all targeted fish species by 2048. Already more than half of the ocean's surface is impacted by industrial fishing. This is an area approximately four times the landmass covered by agriculture. Billions of dollars in government subsidies underlie this phenomenon. The United States, Japan, Spain, China and South Korea provide the largest subsidies to their fishing fleets. Without these subsidies, the fishing industry would not be viable.

A landmark May 2019 UN report warned that maximum yield from fisheries could decline another 24 percent by the end of the century if business and emissions proceed as usual. This decimation will occur while the world attempts to double food production by 2050 to sustain the growing human population. Food choices, and the policies we implement to regulate those choices, have dire implications on whether life on land or sea is sustainable or collapses.

According to a United Nations report, "Nature's Dangerous Decline", published in May 2019, 1,000,000 species are threatened with extinction.

Meat, dairy, and fish subsidies have incentivized the average U.S. citizen to consume about 200 pounds of secondary "protein" a year. This is more than twice the global average, and nearly twice as much as Americans ate in 1961!

Other losers include hundreds of innocent animals out in snow blizzards, hurricanes, and other impossible situations in which they perish, without their 'owners' giving their welfare a second thought, because they know that the US government will 'compensate' them for their 'economic loss'.

The billions of animals bred and raised for food, who do not vote, or have any pockets, never mind deep pockets, endure excruciatingly painful mutilations, horrific genetic manipulation, unsanitary, disease ridden, and tightly confined conditions in modern animal agriculture.

Their misery is shielded from the public by the animal agriculture-backed "Ag-Gag" legislation. This legislation makes it illegal to film or otherwise expose the deplorable conditions in animal agriculture. The purpose of "Ag-Gag" legislation is to prevent animal agriculture's loss of revenue from those consumers who would be put off from knowing the truth about where their meat, poultry, eggs, and dairy come from. This was accomplished with money paid as political contributions to those in power who can create and enforce this and other legislation.

Another looser is planet Earth. Climate change is one of the most serious global problems faced today. Methane, a greenhouse gas from production of secondary protein, holds heat in the atmosphere almost 100 times more effectively than carbon dioxide from lack of sustainable energy. The massive amount of animal feces produced in factory farms is the largest source of airborne methane in the United States.

Additionally, rainforests being cut and burned down to provide grazing land and land to grow crops to feed to animals raised for protein, also contributes to climate change. Of all agricultural land in the U.S., nearly 80% is used to raise animals for food. More than 260 million acres of U.S. forest have been cleared to create cropland to grow grain to feed farmed animals. Forests have a cooling effect on the earth, which is lost when they are cut down to provide crops or grazing for cattle.

Pollution of air, water and land results from secondary "protein". Runoff from factory farms filled with hormones, antibiotics, and bacteria seep into aquifers, and come back as drinking water. Feces from factory farms is often sprayed on nearby land, making the area uninhabitable. Methane and other gases pollute the air.

It is up to you to decide in which direction you want to go, either enjoy healthful primary "protein" from plants, or join those who buy the myth that secondary protein is somehow healthful and necessary, which it is certainly not true.

Chapter 10
Understanding Zoonotic Diseases

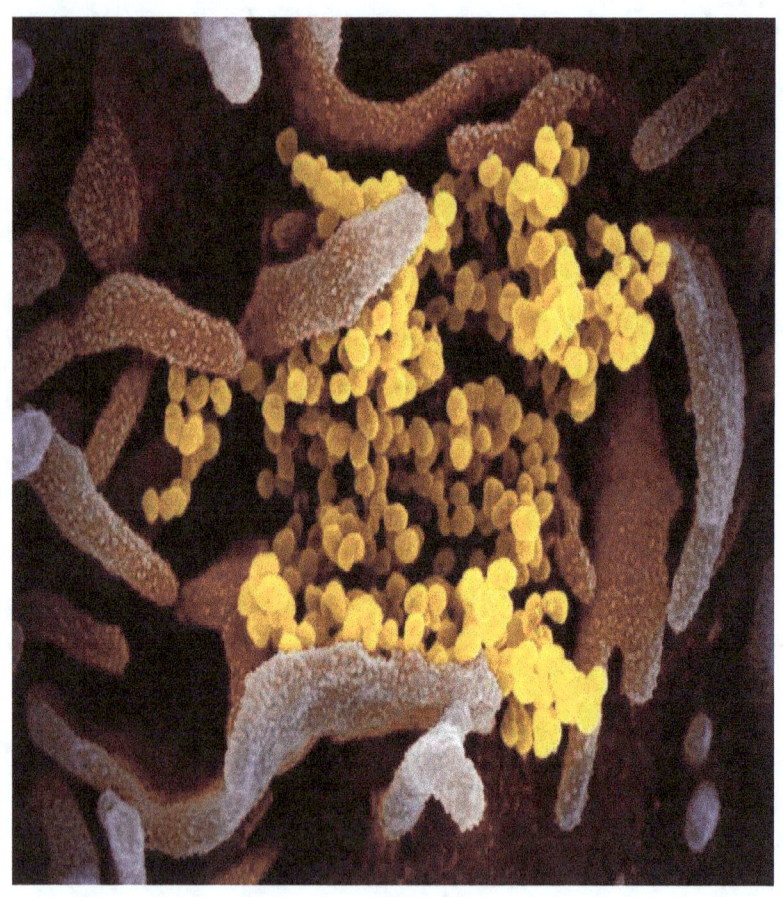

Zoonotic Diseases are the Deadliest Diseases on the Planet

According to the United Nations World Health Organization, animal agriculture and factory farms, the source of the "protein" from meat, poultry, eggs and dairy, is the weakest link in the food chain, and the cause of many illnesses including zoonotic pandemics.

Eating animals, their secretions (milk), and menstruation (eggs), for "protein" is the cause of the non-communicable diseases (NCDs) of heart disease, diabetes, some cancers, obesity and zoonotic diseases, the start of most epidemics and pandemics.

A zoonotic disease, such as Covid-19, HIV AIDS, Monkey Pox, Chicken Pox, Measles, Ebola, Avian Flu, Swine Flu, SARS, MERS, Spanish Flu, Black Flu, the deadliest diseases in the history of the planet, are caused by a pathogen that jumps, or "spills over", from an exploited non-human animal to humans.

Species extinction and habitat destruction has drastically reduced the number of free non-human individuals. Demand for non-human bodies for "protein" has caused the incarcerated non-human population to outnumber the human population by many billions of individuals. This imbalance makes it much more likely for deadly pathogen spill over from animals to humans to occur. Infections and viruses are then transmitted directly among humans.

Globally, the most serious infectious diseases are always zoonotic, causing an estimated 3 million human deaths per year even before the Covid-19 pandemic. Emerging diseases are almost invariably zoonotic. An estimated 60% of all viruses that infect humans came from exploited animals, and 75% of all new infectious diseases in the past decade are zoonotic.

Zoonoses have caused the deadliest pandemics in history: Black Death, Spanish Flu, Swine Flu, Avian Flu, Measles, Ebola, SARS, MERS, Human Immunodeficiency Virus (HIV), and now Covid-19, as well as many others. The global rate and severity of zoonotic disease is increasing. Without understanding the root cause of zoonoses – exploiting and eating animals for secondary protein - and rectifying this, it is impossible to prevent the future pandemics.

HIV/AIDS, also from zoonotic origins, is one of the most serious public health threats of the 21st century. HIV/AIDS originated when an established SIV switched from primates to humans through exposure to blood or other secretions of infected primates. This occurred through the hunting and butchering of innocent wild animals to be used as 'bush meat' for "protein".

Avian (Bird) Flu (H5N1) in 1997, and Swine (Pig) Flu (H1N1) in 2009 emerged from agricultural facilities - factory farms - with horrific conditions. H5N1 has an estimated mortality rate of 60 percent and could easily mutate and become more lethal. H1N1 is believed to have originated in pigs unjustly incarcerated in factory farms in North Carolina. It resulted in more than 200,000 infections and 18,000 human deaths, including 250 children.

Much higher casualties were suffered by the innocent, exploited pigs and birds raised for human 'protein'! According to the UN World Health Organization (WHO), the 1997 outbreak of H5N1 resulted in the death of an estimated 1.5 million chickens and other birds.

The infamous 'Great Influenza' of 1918 – 19, also zoonotic, sickened one-third of the world's population and resulted in the death of over 50 million people. The cause was the horrific exploitation of domestic and wild birds eaten by humans for secondary "protein".

Modern food production involves billions of high-risk interactions between humans and animals. Innocent, incarcerated animals in the food system are relentlessly stressed, confined, forced to share space with dead or diseased animals, share bodily fluids and airborne pathogens, expel waste on each other, all while being fed a steady diet of food laced with antibiotics to prevent loss of profit from their untimely deaths. The physiological stress that animals endure weakens their immune systems making them much more likely to become vectors of disease. The eating animals for 'protein' concept invites deadly zoonotic disaster and other human health hazards.

Factory farms, where most of your 'protein' comes from, are epicenters of disease for humans as well as the billions of unfortunate individual animals involuntarily incarcerated there. Thousands of genetically similar animals are packed together in unsanitary, overcrowded spaces. These unfortunate individuals are vulnerable to disease and stress by these horrific conditions.

An estimated 99% of the ten billion land animals murdered for 'protein' every year in the US alone are imprisoned in factory farms, and murdered with impunity. Innocent animals on Factory Farms, Confined Animal Feeding Operations (CAFOs) or in live markets are severely stressed, cannot engage in natural behaviors, experience frustration, and maladaptive behaviors such as injuring or murdering one another or committing suicide. Pigs can drop dead from the stress of being confined, the only way out of their predicament.

All these conditions make animals (amplifier hosts) more susceptible to pathogens, which then get passed on to their human abusers (bridge population), and then to the human population in general through zoonotic pandemics which are a directly result of the insatiable human desire for unhealthy and inhumane secondary 'protein'.

Eighty percent of the antibiotics produced worldwide are fed to unjustly incarcerated animals raised to be consumed by humans for 'protein'. As a result, humans suffer antibiotic resistant infections, with many resulting in mortality. This is in addition to the unparalleled and inexcusable suffering caused to the sentient beings of other species who are forced to endure this insanity to be someone else's 'protein'. It is now well established that abuse of antibiotics fosters new antibiotic resistant diseases for which people will eventually have no defense. According to the United Nations World Health Organization, 'We are headed for a post-antibiotic era, in which common infections and minor injuries can once again kill.'

Zoonotic disease is preventable. All it takes is recognition that individuals of all species, not just the human species, should be treated justly and the determination to implement that justice.

Chapter 11
Earth's Limited Resources

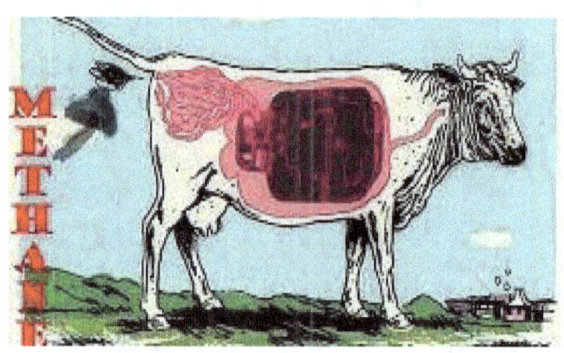

Climate Change from greenhouse gasses is the single greatest threat to the survival of planet Earth today. Methane, the greenhouse gas from animals raised for 'protein', holds heat in the atmosphere more effectively than carbon monoxide.

Meat, dairy, eggs, and fish 'protein' is simply not sustainable. We may not like to admit it, but we are living on a planet with limited resources. The limited resources of land, water, fuel, air, and climate are adversely affected by obtaining secondary 'protein' from other sentient beings.

Land is limited, so rainforests are cut down to provide grazing land for animals raised for 'protein'. Without the cooling effect of forests, this only further exacerbates climate change, and causes land degradation and desertification. It requires twenty times more land to feed a meat-eater than to feed a vegan. 45% of earth's total land is devoted to raising animals for food.

Water - more water is used to produce a pound of meat than a pound of grain. Raising animals for food consumes nearly half the water used in the United States. It takes 2,500 gallons of water to produce a pound of beef, but only 25 gallons to produce a pound of wheat according to People for the Ethical Treatment of Animals.

Fuel is limited. We all want fossil fuel to last forever, but by its very nature, it is limited, and we are slow to switch to solar, wind, and biofuel for energy. More than one-third of all the raw materials, and non-renewable fossil fuels used in the United States, is required to raise animals for food. This includes fuel to produce fertilizer for the crops that are fed to animals, gas and oil to run the trucks that take them to slaughter, electricity to freeze their carcasses, and much more. Additionally, these flesh and blood, sentient creatures are killed in ways that would horrify any compassionate person.

Climate Change mainly caused by methane has far reaching consequences which most people do not even think about. A hotter world is a hungrier, dirtier, more violent world! Raising animals for meat, dairy and egg "protein" expels methane into the atmosphere which holds heat more effectively than carbon dioxide. This causes polar ice caps to melt, and the rising ocean water is eroding coastal areas and small island nations, making them uninhabitable.

Pollution: meat and dairy "protein" is dirty! The meat and dairy industries cause more pollution in the United States than all other industries combined. The United States Environmental Protection Agency (US EPA) reports that chicken, hog, and cattle excrement have polluted 35,000 miles of rivers in 22 states, and contaminated groundwater in 17 states. The meat industry causes more water pollution in the United States than all other industries combined. Animals raised for food produce 130 times more excrement than the entire human population does – 86,000 pounds per second. A typical pig factory farm generates a quantity of raw waste equal to that of a city of 50,000 people, but without the sewage system. Instead, this excrement seeps into ground water, and is often sprayed on land. Water and air are being hopelessly polluted usually with little or no regulation or consequences for the polluters. Adverse health consequences result, usually in the neighborhoods of the underprivileged

Habitat destruction caused by animal agriculture is the number one cause of wildlife habitat loss, and species extinction.

Wild animals are losing their populations at unprecedented rates due to human activity. Reducing wildlife habitat increases the number and frequency of zoonotic pandemics by reducing the 'dilution effect' and increasing the 'spill-over effect'.

Hunger, starvation and malnutrition are caused by the meat and dairy "protein" diet choice of the affluent. More than 80% of starving and hungry children live in countries where food is grown and exported to feed animals raised for food. 3.5 billion more people could be fed by growing plants for human consumption on land currently used to grow crops for farmed animal 'protein'.

In addition to health and environmental reasons to rethink secondary 'protein' there are other reasons, specifically, those individuals who are considered by some to be 'protein'. The largest number of exploited, tortured, murdered individuals on earth today are animals: domestic or wild, in the air, on land, and in the water.

Chapter 12
Dairy Is Scary

Dairy has been linked to Heart Disease, Diabetes- both Type One and Type Two - Testicular Cancer in men, Premature Menstruation in Girls, Breast Cancer in Women, Obesity, and Lactose Intolerance, among others.

This is where dairy comes from - to produce milk, dairy cows must give birth.

Dairy "protein" starts with bestiality. A steer, castrated male, is immobilized with metal bars to be used as a 'teaser'. A male bull is forced to mount the steer. When he gets an erection, humans pull him off, and manually ejaculated the violated bull. This liquid is ultimately sold to dairy companies to be used in the rape of immobilized cows and heifers, young female cattle who have never had a baby.

Dairy 'protein' involves Artificial Insemination, 'AI'. A farm worker, not a Veterinarian, inserts his arm up to his elbow in the terrified cow's rectum. This is completely unnatural and causes an uncontrollable and painful bowel movement. Then the uterus is manually turned to make it susceptible to impregnation.

When a cow is raped, first the worker inserts his arm up to the elbow in the cow's rectum. This is never done in nature and usually causes uncontrollable diarrhea. The cow's uterus is turned to make it ready to accept the 'gun' – similar to a calk gun – full of bull fluid. If this does not impregnate the cow, it fiasco, is done repeatedly until the cow becomes pregnant. The cow is giving milk multiple times a day during this fiasco.

A 'gun' filled with the bull's sperm is forced into the cow's vagina in rape like fashion. If the cow does not become pregnant from the rape, this horrific procedure is done repeatedly. This is done annually.

These procedures would be considered 'bestiality' outside of the dairy industry, and the crime of rape if done to a human. Like with humans, the rape is extremely painful both physically and psychologically for the innocent sentient cow.

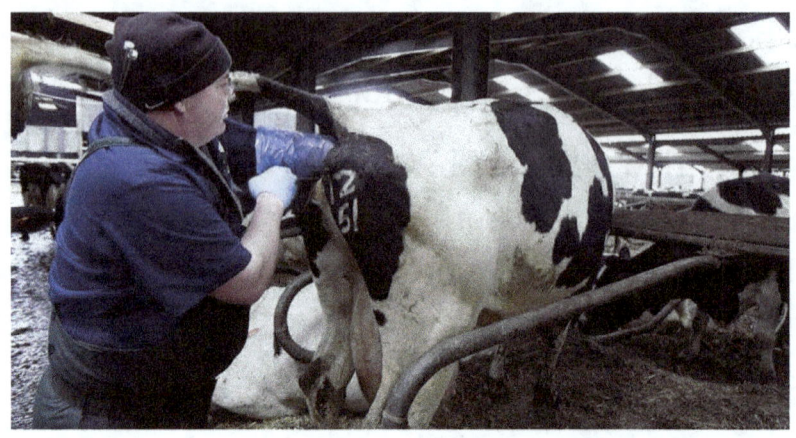

Note: the bladder is so full it is down to the floor and they are impregnating/raping the cow again. Where are the previous babies? Note the numbers tattooed right on the cow's skin and her immobilized position. This guy is a worker with no medical training inserting his arm up to the elbow in the Cow's rectum to turn her uterus which never happens in nature and will cause suffering and uncontrollable defecation.

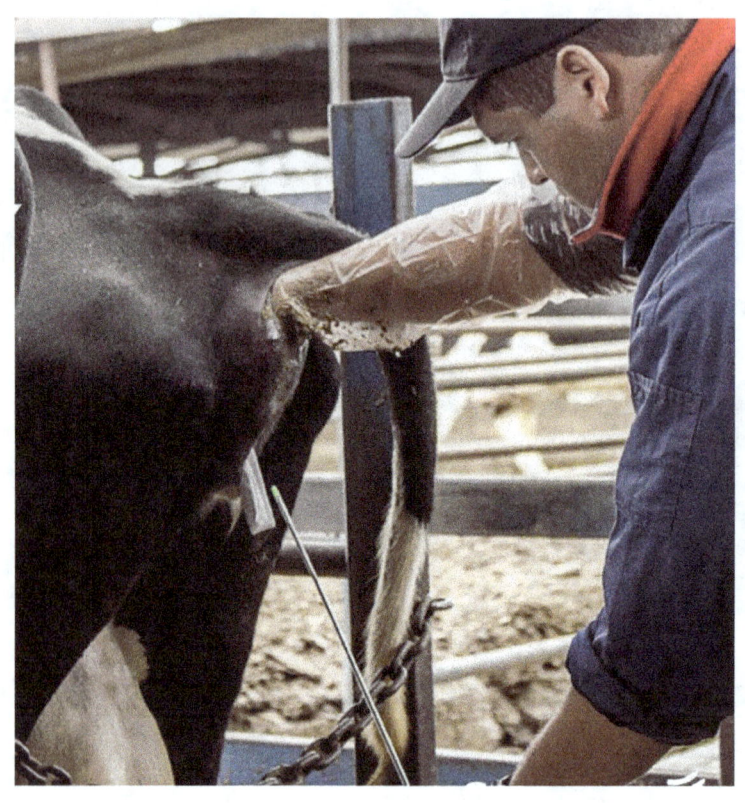

Note the metal rod held by the human to beat the cow into submission during the rape.

To produce milk, dairy cows must give birth.

During pregnancy, the cows endure a physically demanding nine-month gestation period, during which time they are forced to give milk for the first seven months.

During her pregnancy, the cows is forced to give milk which was meant for her previous baby. When the current pregnancy has come to term, the human interference is traumatic and horrific.

Note the torture involved and the large bladder full of milk from previous births. This Mother is unlikely to see her baby ever again. He will be murdered for veal if he is a boy, and isolated and fed 'formula' until old enough to be raped if she is a girl.

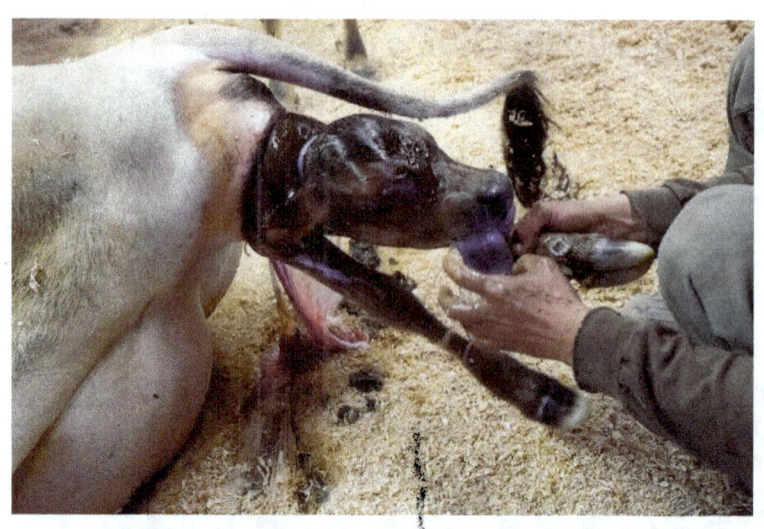

Another Mother being used to produce milk constantly even while pregnant. She is giving birth to a baby she will never see again and will mourn for.

Cows are Mothers. In all species, Mothers love their babies, and babies need their Mothers. These Mothers have been forcefully and brutally raped, and their babies stolen from them. They grieve inconsolably for their babies.

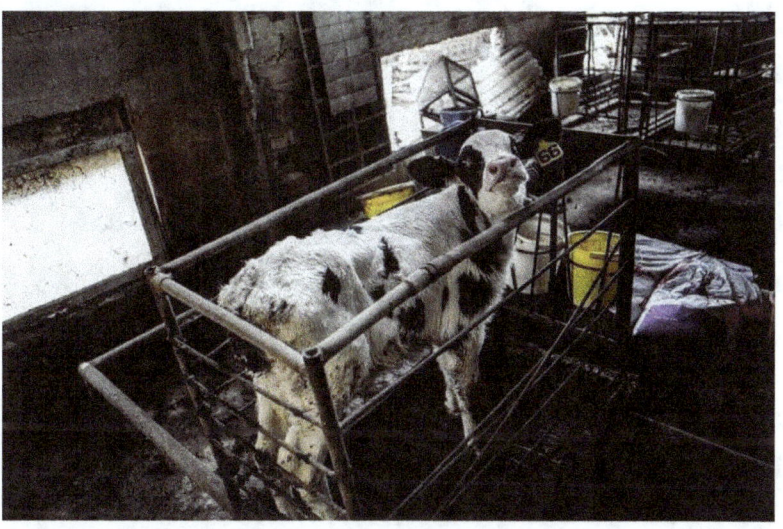

Most baby boys are brutally slaughtered. This day-old baby boy is no use in the dairy industry. He will be murdered as a dairy 'waste product' or live a short, tortured life as a 'veal calf'.

Veal calves are a "by-product" of the dairy industry. Baby boy calves are not able to produce milk, so they are taken from their mothers, chained by the neck, and kept in crates so small they cannot turn around, stretch, or lie down. Their muscles are not able to develop, keeping their flesh 'tender'. They are fed a poor diet, making them anemic. These sick, abused animals produce pale-colored flesh. The inhumane conditions cause the calves to be more likely to develop diseases than cattle would in more normal circumstances. Veal calves requires copious amounts of medication to keep them alive until slaughter at a few months of age. Veal is the most likely meat to contain illegal drug residues which pose a threat to humans consuming it for "protein".

Newborn Baby Boy has been taken from his Mother. They will never see each other again. Her milk will be stolen and sold and he will be murdered as a 'waste product' or tortured as 'veal'.

The baby girls are fed a type of formula until they are just barely old enough to become Mothers themselves. Then they are raped, tortured, tormented, and forced to produce milk.

Here is her isolated baby girl in winter freezing to death and in summer literally cooking to death. She is eating artificial 'formula' until she is old enough to be raped herself.

if you've "got milk" it's because they don't.

Isolated baby girls taken from their Mothers and fed 'formula' until old enough to be raped.

Frightened, confused and desperate for their mothers, these baby girls are often isolated in rickety cramped enclosures, and left outside in the harsh environment, laying in mud and their own feces. The calves often face peril from prolonged exposures to the extremities of the weathering heat and inclement weather. Usually, if cover is provided, it is in the form of disintegrating, shredded tarps or plastic hutches where they cook in summer and freeze in winter.

171

After the birth and kidnap of their beloved baby, the Mother Cow is milked. These Mothers are tortured, beaten into submission, kept in filthy conditions, and repeatedly raped during their short lives.

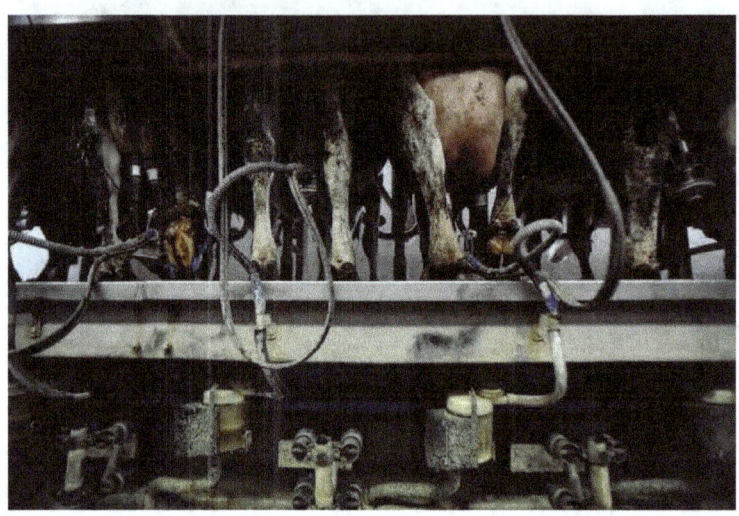

Milking is done by machines and is very painful physically and psychologically for the cows. There is no effort to provide hygiene. Mother Cows are milked by machines in filthy conditions.

Dairy cows live short, confined lives of repeated rapes by male workers. In addition, these innocent exploited individual cows endure unnatural feeds, painful injections, and calcium depleted bones.

These Mothers give birth to a calf a year. Their beloved baby is always taken away from them soon after birth. Mother cows mourn the loss of their baby calves and bellow mournfully for weeks.

With genetic mutation, cows produce 100 pounds of milk a day – ten times more than in nature. Their udders are so heavy and swollen that they are in constant pain and are unable to walk properly. Hormones banned in Europe and Canada are used in the United States to increase milk production. This causes birth defects in the calves.

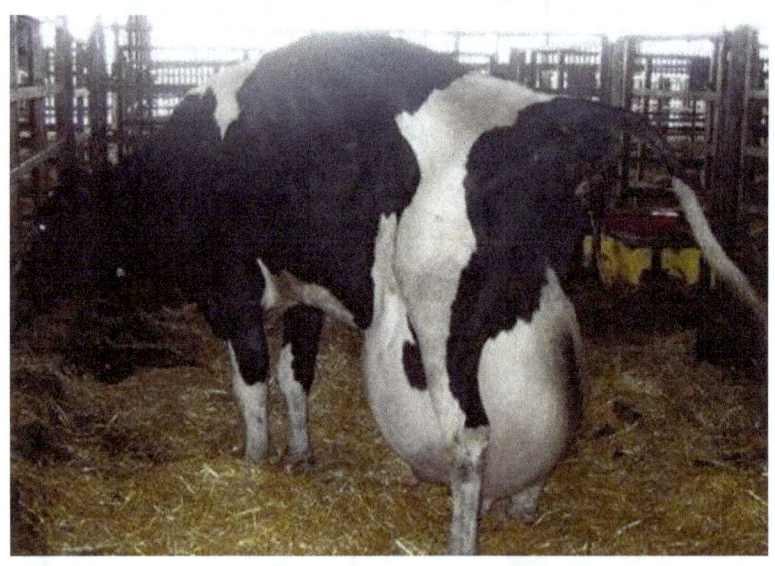

174

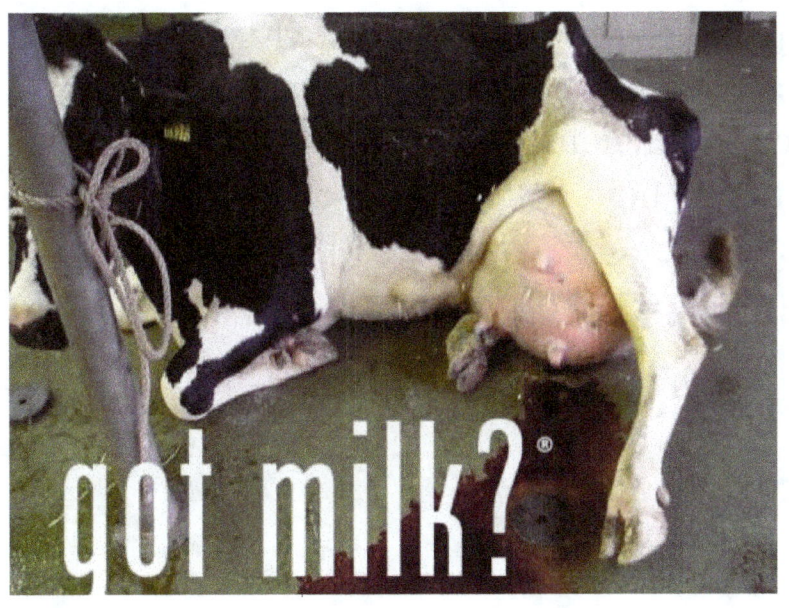

The oversize bladders are due to hormones banned in most countries. They force the cow's body to produce hundreds of times the normal amount of milk. This is painful physically as well as mentally and emotionally for the individuals. In addition, these hormones are passed on to the humans who drink the milk causing premature puberty in girls, a possible causative factor in breast cancer in both women and men and being the number one cause of the epidemic of testicular cancer in human men. These dangerous hormones are especially concentrated in ice cream and cheese while there are delicious non-dairy alternatives of plant milk, non- dairy cheese, and non-dairy ice cream.

Treatment of Cows while being milked.

An undercover investigation of Fairlife Dairy in Florida by Animal Rescue Mission (ARM) in June 2019 revealed that cows live in over cramped holding barns during the 305 days a year of the milk production phase. They overheat and collapse from exhaustion due to the extremely poor living conditions and insufficient ventilation. Cows are ridiculed and tormented as they are maneuvered to the milk production lines. Electrical prods and violent excessive force are used.

Cows are beaten into submission with metal construction rods. Undercover agents documented several forms of home-made torture tools, including a spear-like weapon, that are used to repeatedly stab the Mothers in the ribs, inflicting wounds that are left untreated. They are also beaten over their heads and bodies with these rods. As a result of the continuous and forceful beatings, the cows fall to the ground.

During daily milk collections, cows are beaten over the head, punched, poked, and kicked, including in their sensitive udders, with primitive tools, hooks and tools. These beatings usually occur while the frightened animals are trapped in a metal headlock and unable to escape. The cows were witnessed to be maliciously beaten repeatedly for no apparent reason and deep wounds and untreated abrasions were evident.

During milking, workers are *taught* to grab the cows' tails and forcefully bend/fold and possibly break the tail bones. The logic for this is unclear.

Milk is collected from the cows three times a day. This means the animals are being subjected to major stress, discomfort, pain, torture and suffering three times a day, 365 days of the year. Through this investigation, it became clear that the workers have an unwavering and deep hatred for the dairy cows, and that the beatings relay an inferior respect of the animals' welfare and rights to life.

Outside of the milking and holding barns, the abuse continues with the calves – considered as mere bi-products of the dairy industry. Sadly, the protocols on dairy farms are to rip the babies away from their Mothers, sometimes as they are born. On the dairy farm, the mistreatment of the newborn calves is evident.

This is 'udder burning' done with a blow torch on the cows' painful, over exploited, sensitive udders. Supposedly it is to remove hair from the udders. In nature, there is no problem with hair on the cow's body. This is more likely another way to force cows into submission by 'showing them who's boss' which is very common in animal agriculture.

Milk from this investigated dairy is sold in my supermarket. I contacted my supermarket headquarters with a copy of the report and request that the supermarket discontinue selling this milk. It did not happen, no doubt due to financial reasons. Exploited cows have no financial power, only the milk drinking consumers do.

Is organic dairy better? Not at all! A visit to an organic dairy farm in California was documented by Robert Grillo, Founder of 'Free From Harm'. I invite you to read his report on the FreeFromHarm.org website. It is one of the most heart-breaking things you will ever read.

The cows are fed unnatural diets which cause disease, some of which are fatal. All dairy cows suffer from diseases directly related to the way they are treated. In nature, cows live about 20 years, in the dairy industry, they are 'unproductive', 'spent', and slaughtered at about three or four years old. Due to repeatedly being impregnated, she becomes "spent" and therefore an economic liability to farmers, who then send her to slaughter. All of this is done without the animal understanding why she is being violated or why her babies are being taken from her.

"Downed cows" are worn out, depleted dairy cows who are so weak, and diseased from the lives they have been forced to live, that they cannot stand. These "downers" are still sold for human consumption. They are typically left without food, water, or care, for days until it is convenient to take them to slaughter. Usually they are moved by the most convenient, least humane ways, such as being dragged or pushed with tractors or forklifts. This causes even more suffering and injuries. Downed animals are not protected from abuse under federal animal welfare laws, no matter how cruel the treatment is. They are slaughtered in horrific ways, and become low grade hamburger, and low-quality beef products.

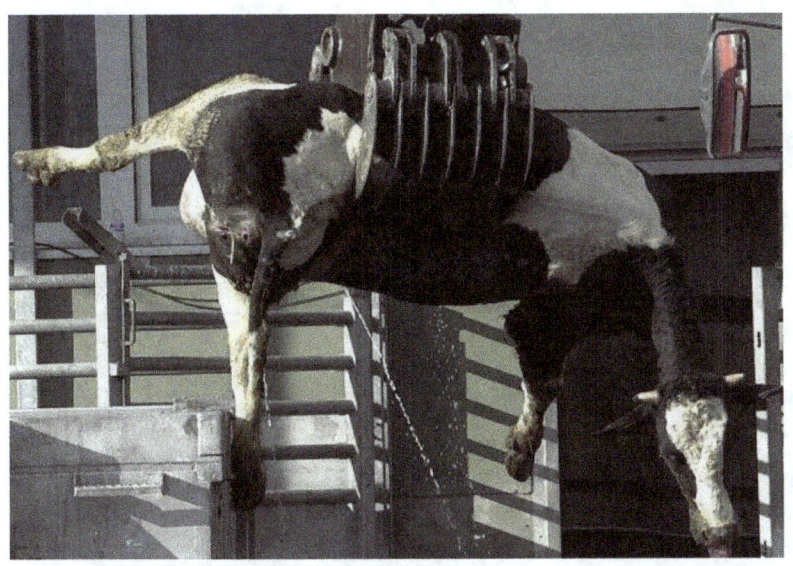

Note the horrible way of transporting a cow to keep her alive so that she is murdered in the slaughter facility to keep her body 'fresh' for hamburger meat.

No painkillers or therapeutic medication of any kind is administered, except antibiotics used to prolong life in unsanitary conditions. Note the excrement on the cow's legs from being confined in her own feces.

185

Dairy cows live short, confined lives of repeated rapes by male workers. In addition, these innocent exploited individual cows endure unnatural feeds, painful injections, and calcium depleted bones. These Mothers give birth to a calf a year. Their beloved baby is taken from them soon after birth. Mother cows mourn the loss of their baby calves and can bellow mournfully for weeks.

"Spent" cows are brutally slaughtered after their short lives filled with endless sorrow and pain. There is a deep injustice in dairy. For your sake and theirs, please don't think of these innocent suffering individuals as dairy "protein"!

The dairy industry is notorious for horrific treatment of the individuals it exploits. This includes the supposedly 'humane' and 'organic' dairy. There is no humane way to rape and kidnap individuals. There is no benefit to humans from consuming excretions from other species. Countless human scientific studies prove this.

If this is not enough to convince you not to use dairy for protein, consider this: dairy has been linked to the non-communicable diseases of diabetes, heart disease, obesity, some cancers, and obesity as well as lactose intolerance, and has been proven not to be a good source of calcium. Scientific studies at Harvard prove individuals consuming dairy 'protein' break more bone than those who do not consume dairy.

Chapter 13
Eggs A Good Source Of Cholesterol
Not "Protein"

This is a Mother Hen and her Baby Chick in nature.

Eggs, a hen's menstrual cycle, are probably the highest source of cholesterol available. Fat and cholesterol have been linked to most diseases including heart disease, diabetes, and cancer.

Cage-free, free-range, and organic, are marketing terms used to sell cholesterol laden eggs to consumers who erroneously believe that these eggs are somehow 'healthful' and guilt free. Nothing could be further from the truth.

Eggs are unfertilized by roosters because the male chicks are destroyed as chicks by huge agribusiness corporations. Male chicks are of no use to the egg industry. Newborn baby male chicks are thrown into plastic garbage bags. They suffocate slowly under the weight of the other chicks dumped on top of them, or are pulverized in machines designed to grind them up alive. Male chicks are also ground up for animal feed while still alive.

In the Egg Industry, baby boys are not profitable, so they are murdered on the day of their birth or the following day. They are either suffocated in large garbage bags or put in grinding machines and made into fertilizer while alive.

Ground up day old male chicks.

The male chicks are not treated any better in organic, cage-free, or free-range, than the conventional egg industry. These unwanted, unprofitable, vulnerable individuals are murdered, often hours after birth, by the same methods as conventional male chicks.

While the male chicks are murdered soon after birth, the female chicks are mutilated. To prevent cannibalism, hens are debeaked. A hot blade cuts through bone, cartilage, and soft tissue without benefit of pain relief. The sensitive beak, comparable to the human fingertip, is removed to prevent these babies from committing suicide by pecking themselves to death, eliminating profits. Many birds die from shock during the process.

Newborn girls being 'debeaked'.

A beak is as sensitive as a human fingertip. Beaks are removed to prevent hens from committing suicide or murder from the horrific conditions they will be forced to endure during their short lives. The loss of hens would cause a loss of profit. Animal agriculture's focus is always on human profit. Eggs are loaded with cholesterol, a serious human health threat, but the focus is on human dollars and not human health

In nature, Mother Hens keep all their baby chicks –both boys and girls – safe under their wings until they are old enough to venture out alone.

Huge agribusiness corporations produce eggs, both the conventional and specialty eggs. All hens are kept in crowded battery cages where their most basic instincts are cruelly violated. There is no natural light. There are four or five hens in each cage. They cannot walk or stretch their wings. Their feathers fall out, their skin becomes raw and often bloody, and their feet are injured, and often caught, by the wire floor. When the hen's feet become caught in the wire floor, it can prevent her from reaching food. Hens can slowly starve to death inches from food. Dead hens remain in the cage with living hens. Even 'cage-free' or 'free range' hens are kept by the thousands in buildings the size of football fields violating their natural instincts and inviting disease for themselves and those who eat their eggs for 'protein'.

The egg industry uses enormous amounts of antibiotics, pesticides, and other chemicals. The organic egg industry uses "organic' products which are in reality just as harmful. Pesticides are fed to the hens so that their excrement attracts fewer flies. Eggs yolks are chemically dyed to achieve a yellow look, which in nature comes from the sun. All of this is physically and psychologically harmful to the exploited hens.

When egg production falls off, the industry starves, and denies hens water, for several days. This 'forced molting' shocks the hens into losing whatever feathers they have left, and starts a new egg laying cycle. Many hens die during this tortuous cycle. There is no veterinary care. Still alive, but dying hens are thrown on 'dead piles' with the already dead hens.

Conventional Eggs Come From Here

This is conventional egg production. It looks very sanitary doesn't it? The yellow yolk color in nature comes from the sun. In animal agriculture it comes from the yellow dye fed to the hens. The hens are also fed poison to kill the flies who would normally infest the feces. The hens are also starved to force a 'molt' or new menstrual cycle for more eggs. All this bad karma and exorbitant amounts of cholesterol is in the eggs you eat.

Cage Free facilities often house several thousand birds in a single building. They cannot walk around, fly, groom themselves, or engage in any natural behavior. They live in feces and urine, and breath ammonia not air. But they are 'cage free'.

Cage Free Hens and Eggs

Free range is no better. These caring, affectionate, intelligent beings are not protected by any laws or regulations defining 'free range'. Free range is anything the profit driven producer wants it to be. This is a marketing term used to sell products to uninformed consumers, not a way to treat the hens better.

This is a typical 'free range', 'humane', or organic situation. There are no laws regulating advertising, terminology, or incarceration. Many free-range hens are kept in buildings the size of football fields and never go outside. There is no oversight even if advertising convinces the consumer otherwise.

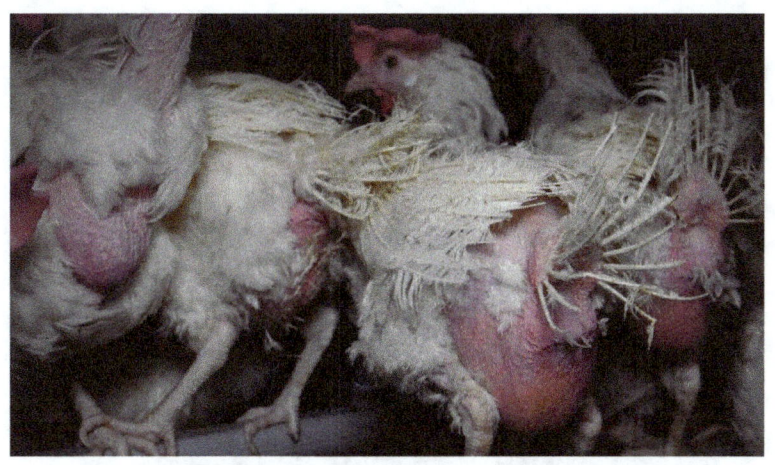

More Free-Range Hens.

Organic only refers to the food the birds eat. All other horrific circumstances of their short horrific lives, and inhumane slaughter are the same. Organic is about profit; it is not about compassion or health.

Modern egg production involves artificially forcing the individual Mother's bodies to produce more menstrual periods (eggs) than is intended by nature.

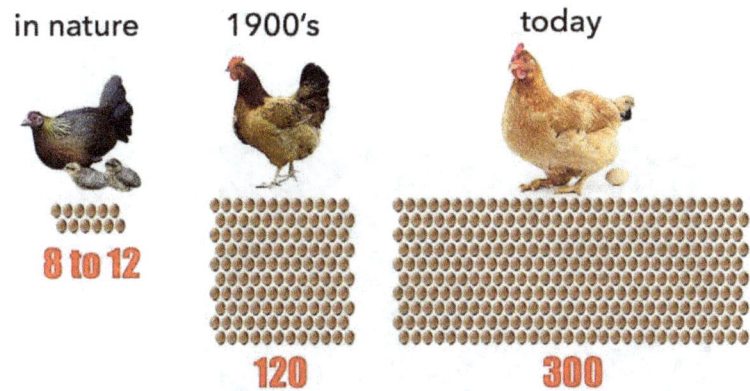

In nature, hens produce approximately ten eggs a year, and only during the breeding season. Commercial egg laying hens are forced to produce up to 300 eggs a year. This is done by forcing molting, or painfully starving the hens into a new cycle in their bodies.

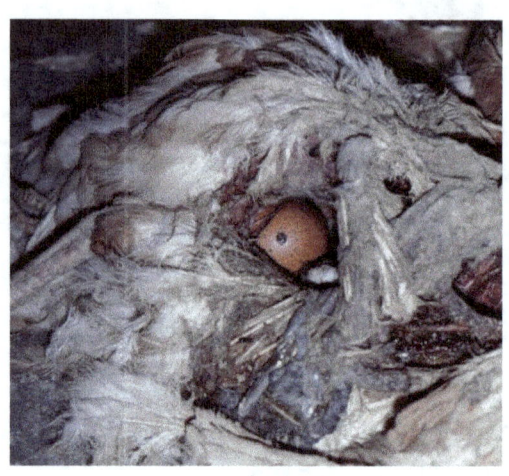

Eggs can become trapped in the hens' bodies. Since there is never any Veterinary help for these animals, the eggs are 'cooked' in the hens' bodies. This causes the hens to perish in a horrible and painful death.

This is what a Mother Hen looks like after you have eaten all her menstrual cycles.

Hens usually live 10 to 15 years in nature. In the egg industry the hens live a year to a year and a half before their bodies give out.

There is nothing nice about the egg industry

When egg production falls off, the industry starves, and denies hens water, for several days. This 'forced molting' shocks the hens into losing whatever feathers they have left, and starts a new egg laying cycle. Many hens die during this tortuous cycle. There is no veterinary care. Still alive, but dying hens are thrown on 'dead piles' with the already dead hens.

The egg industry kills TWELVE BILLION birds a year, SIX BILLION whose bodies are so exhausted they can't produce anymore eggs and SIX BILLION are shredded alive at one or two days old for being male, and unprofitable for the egg industry.

These innocent birds are going to slaughter with no protection from the elements: freezing or sweltering conditions. This is the first time they have seen daylight in their lives.

Hens are sentient beings not protected by the federal Human Slaughter Law. Those very limited protections are reserved for mammals - animals, who like humans, produce milk for their young. This restriction exists because humans can 'relate' to mammals more than to hens, not because the birds are any less deserving of protection.

Birds, and other non-mammals, are slaughtered in the most horrific ways. The focus is on profits, not compassion. These two are mutually exclusive, and no slaughter is "humane".

Eggs are neither healthful nor humane. They are a tremendous source of both disease-producing cholesterol and unimaginable cruelty. It is best to avoid egg "protein".

Chapter 14 Meet Your Bacon

Bacon is a very popular source of "protein" for some humans. But it is not only unhealthy for a host of reasons, but also one of the most horrific acts of violence and depravity on earth.

Bacon "protein" comes from pigs: Sows (Mothers), Boars (Fathers) and Piglets (Babies), approximately one hundred million, are raised and slaughtered in the United States every year. In nature, pigs live in social groups in light woodlands. Pigs are one of the most intelligent and affectionate animals on earth. They are naturally very clean, and very active. Pregnant sows build large nests where they give birth and protect their piglets

Undercover investigations reveal that when these docile, loving creatures are raised for food they are subjected to the most egregious abuses imaginable. For example, semen is collected from the boars by means that should be considered bestiality.

The sows are locked in cages so small that they cannot stand or turn around. They are immobilized like this for their entire short lives. Even in prison solitary confinement, prisoners can stand and walk, but not Mother Pigs.

In this vulnerable position, from which there is no escape, the docile, intelligent, sentient girls are artificially inseminated by workers. These cruel men manipulate the sows' vaginas to insert the semen. Sometimes a boar (male pig), is dragged around by a robot between forced masturbation sessions in the hope that this poor unfortunate's smell will facilitate the heinous procedure. The sweet, gentle sows are then raped repeatedly until conception takes place.

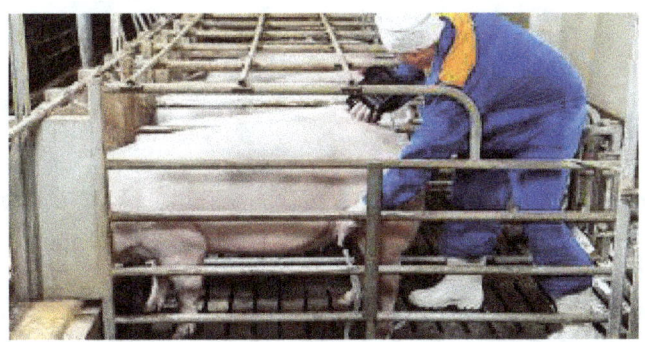

Sow being raped by a worker.

Of all pigs, the breeding sows are treated the most cruelly. They live in a continual cycle of artificial insemination from masturbated male pigs, birth, and re-impregnation. The sows are confined in small, metal gestation crates. For their entire lives, the sows cannot walk or turn around, and barely have room to stand up. They are denied straw bedding and must lie on concrete.

These gentle individuals are forced to endure all this horror so humans can 'enjoy' ham or bacon for 'protein' even though this 'protein' has been linked to obesity, and many other diseases. The red pain indicates individuals who have 'given up' and stopped eating because their only means of escape is death, and their only method of suicide is starvation. They will be sent to slaughter to avoid 'economic loss'.

When the innocent baby pigs are born, they nurse from their incarcerated, pinned down Mothers briefly before being removed by workers. In factory farms, piglets are taken from their grieving Mothers when they are as young as three weeks old. The Mother's and Babies' screams are heartbreaking. The Mothers mourn the loss of their babies, as any other mother would. Their physical, and psychological suffering is immense.

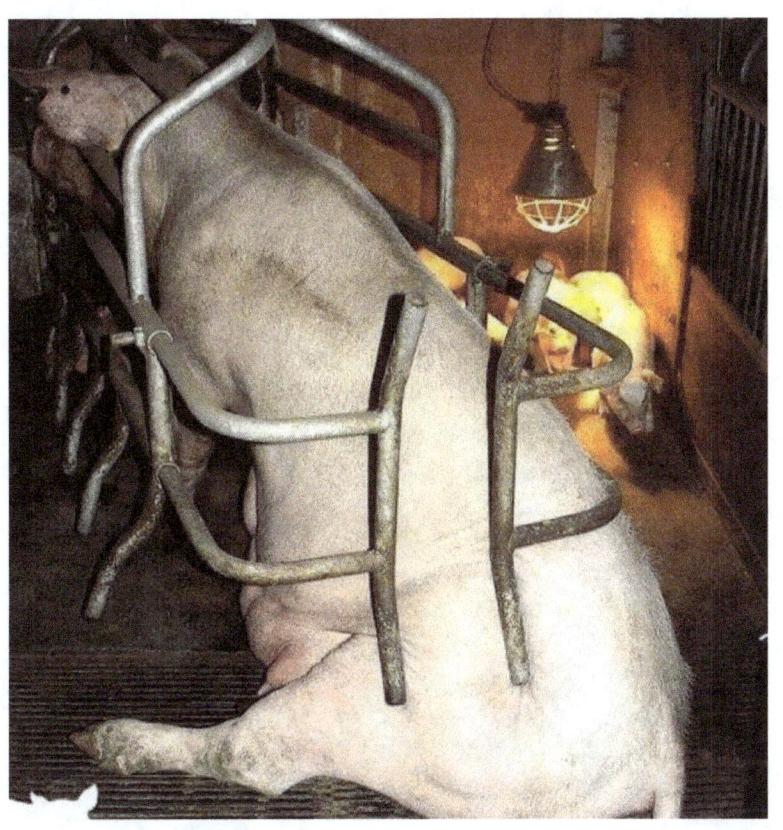

Mother Pig immobilized and separated from her babies who are under a lamp rather than their Mother to keep them warm.

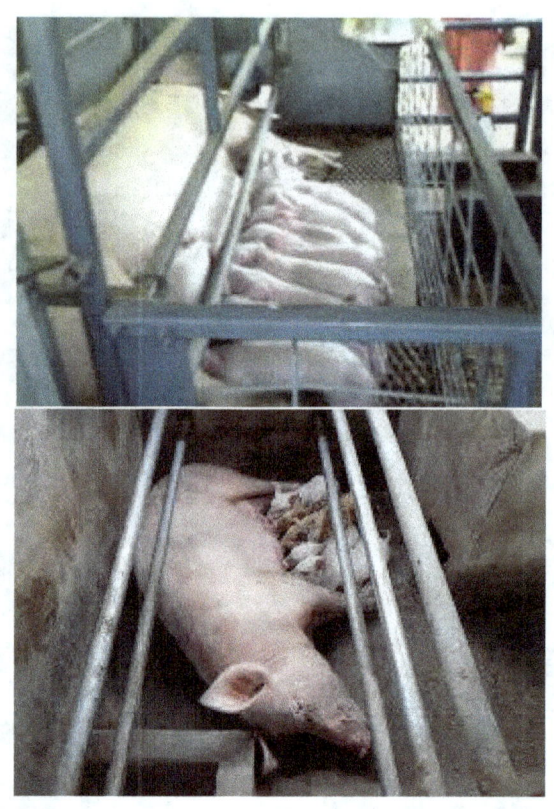

Nursing Mothers completely immobilized

The baby piglets are housed in indoor barren, over-crowded pens. There is no straw or other bedding. They lie on concrete. After piglets are taken from their mothers, their tails are cut off with pliers, or a hot docking iron, without pain relief causing permanent pain.

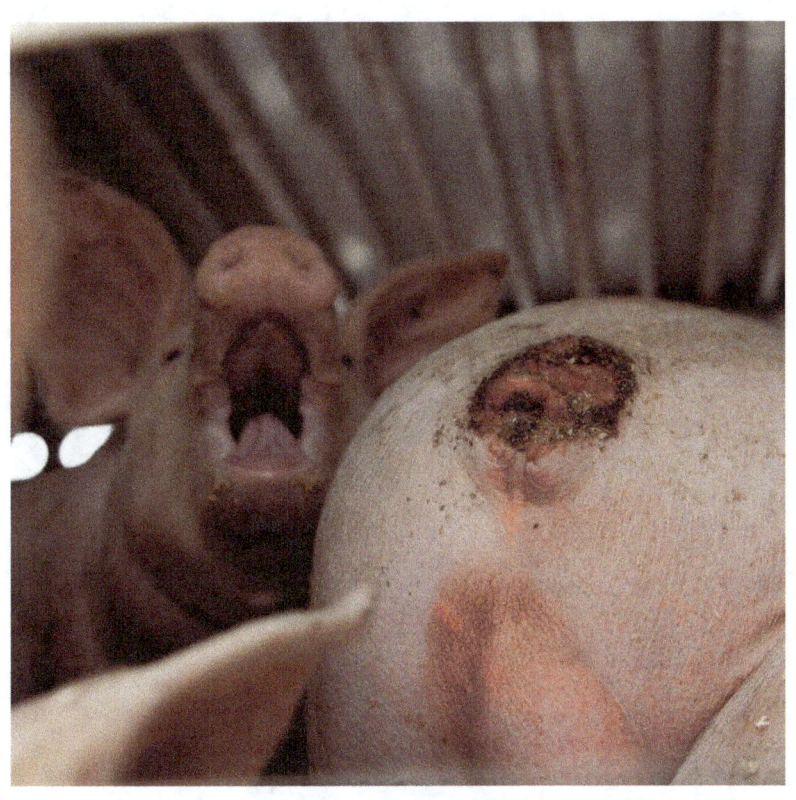

No Tails for Pigs in Animal Agriculture

The baby boy piglets have their testicles removed without anesthesia or pain relief. Their high-pitched screams are heart breaking. Their tails are removed to prevent the natural act of sucking by their companions looking for mother's milk. Their teeth are filed down to prevent 'financial loss' from cannibalism caused by the unbearable circumstances of their short lives. The mutilations cause pain, illness, and even death.

Baby boys being mutilated without pain relief or protection from infection. Their screams are heartbreaking. There is nothing their imprisoned Mothers can do to protect them.

Approximately 15% of the piglets die soon after leaving their mothers. The surviving piglets endure these horrific circumstances until their death at six months of age after they have gained enough weight to be profitable.

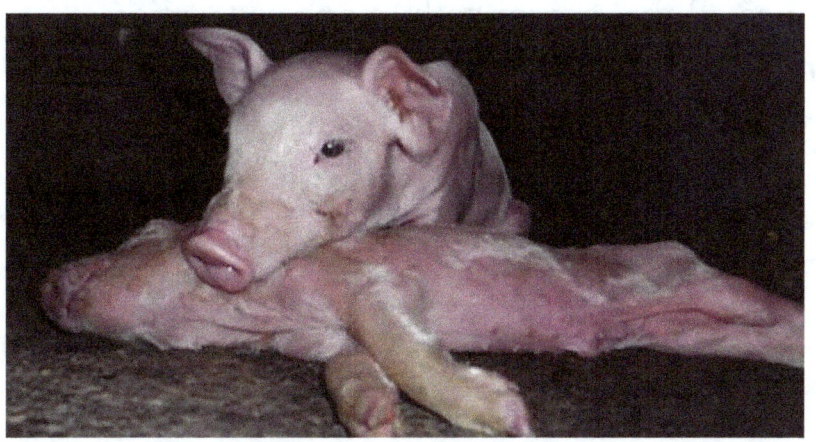

Caring, loving individual grieving for his deceased brother.

Each sow is forced to have 20 piglets per year. After three or four years, the breeding sows often stop eating from depression due to the abuse and are no longer deemed productive. Slaughter/murder comes for the Mothers when they are no longer able to produce babies either because their reproductive organs have been expelled from their bodies, or they have become so hopeless that they stop eating.

These gentle individuals are forced to endure all this horror so humans can 'enjoy' ham or bacon for 'protein' even though this 'protein' has been linked to obesity, and many other diseases.

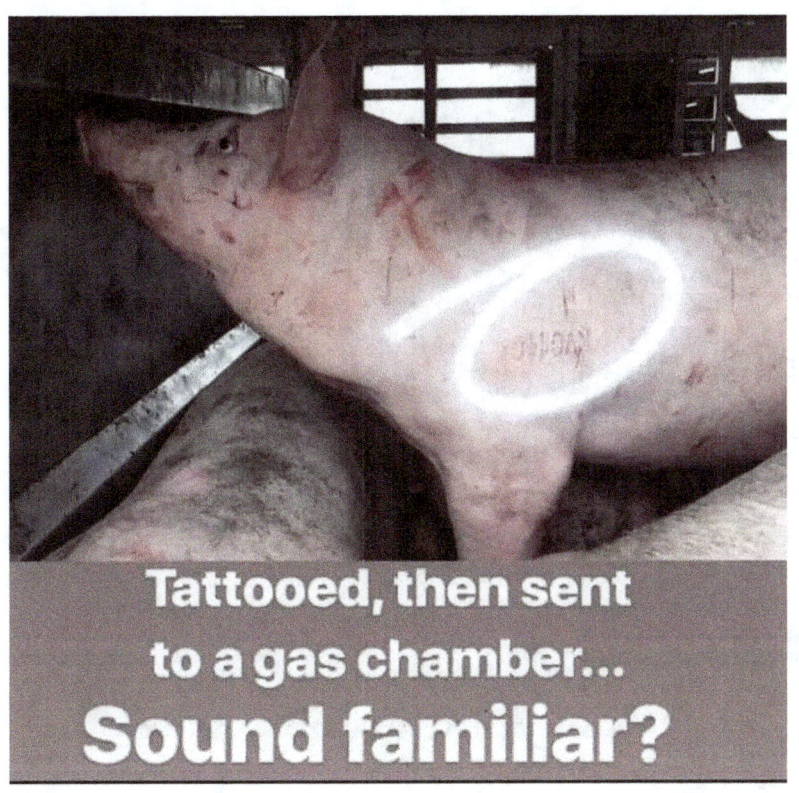

Tattooed, then sent to a gas chamber... Sound familiar?

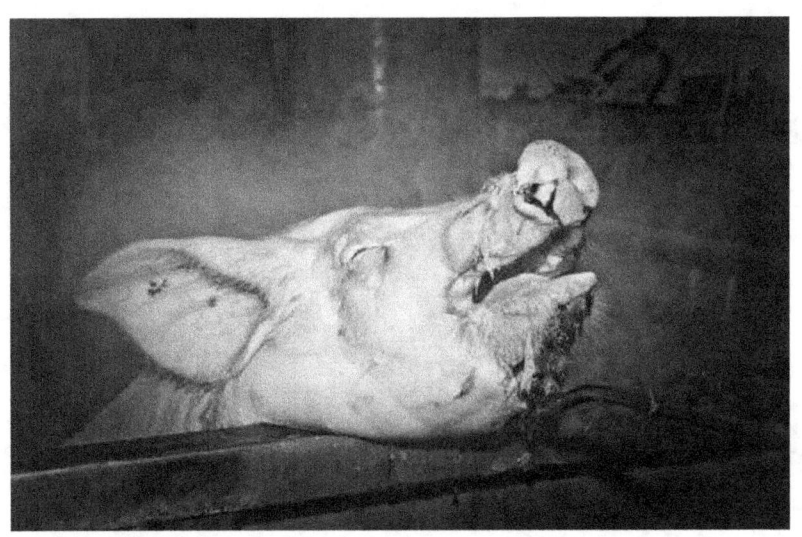

This unfortunate individual is being boiled alive because there are few safeguards and little or no concern in animal agriculture.

This courageous and resourceful individual is smart enough to know his only chance for survival is escape and is willing to endure the risk to survive.

This is a Mother and baby pig in nature.

This is a Mother and baby pig in nature.

Chapter 15:
Animal Agriculture: Source of 'Protein' or Impending Disaster?

"Never forget there's no such thing as 'humane slaughter'. I never saw an animal clicking its heels going to the slaughterhouse, saying 'Yipee, skippy. I'm going to be a McDonald's burger tomorrow!' There is always fear in their eyes. They know exactly what's going to happen. So for anyone to claim there is such a thing as 'humane slaughter', well, that's the greatest oxymoron in the world." Howard Lyman, former 4th generation Cattle Rancher turned Vegan and Activist.

So why not meat, dairy, poultry, eggs and sea animals for 'Protein'? Exploited animals are more than 'protein'. They are innocent individuals who suffer the loss of their children, violation of their bodies, experience fear and pain, are tortured and murdered with impunity, and have absolutely no recourse.

Animal Agriculture causes the death of more than 5 billion pigs, cows, calves, turkeys, and fish each year for 'protein' in the United States alone. On factory farms where most 'protein' animals, dairy, and eggs come from, disease is so prevalent in these conditions that antibiotics are routinely fed to animals causing antibiotic resistance in humans, one of the largest threats to human health today.

More chickens: hens, roosters and chicks, are farmed than any other animal. Over nine billion chickens are murdered for human 'protein' each year. It is approximately one million an hour in the United States alone.

The scale of their suffering is unimaginable. Tens of thousands of these individuals are kept in sheds where there is no natural light. The air is unbreathable due to ammonia from urine. Baby chicks have their beaks and toes cut off to prevent fighting due to extreme overcrowding.

These sentient beings who are raised for meat are genetically altered to grow twice as fast, and twice as large, as normal individuals. This causes a host of health issues, and the unhealthy living conditions expose them to all kinds of disease. These diseases can then be transferred to humans. One of these zoonotic pandemics is Avian Flu. These horrific conditions make many other inter-species pandemic outbreaks possible.

Transportation to slaughter is done by the cheapest means possible. The hens and roosters are packed in crates on the backs of trucks unprotected from weather conditions. Individuals literally freeze to death in winter, or die from heat stress, and suffocation in summer. At the slaughterhouse, which is also referred to as a 'packing' or 'processing' plant, crates of these defenseless individuals are removed from trucks with cranes or forklifts and dumped on a conveyor belt. As the birds are unloaded, some fall on the floor where they die from being crushed by machinery or vehicles, or they die slowly from starvation and neglect.

Fully conscious hens and roosters are hung by their feet on a moving rail. Stunning is not required because birds are not covered by the Humane Slaughter Act. These individuals are killed as cheaply as possible, regardless of the additional suffering it causes. The birds' throats are slashed, usually by a mechanical blade which often misses. Then the dead and the live hens and roosters, are submerged in boiling water. Birds missed by the killing blade are boiled alive. This is such a common occurrence that they are called 'redskins'.

Hen and Tom Turkeys are slaughtered at the rate of about 300 million a year. Most are raised in confinement. Disease and suffering are rampant in these inhumane conditions. Stressed turkeys are driven to fighting, causing 'economic' loss. To prevent 'loss', the turkey's beaks and toes are cut off without pain relief. Turkeys have been anatomically manipulated to grow abnormally fast and large.

If a seven-pound baby grew at the same rate as the turkeys are forced to, the baby would weigh 1500 pounds at 18 weeks of age. When the hens and toms reach market weight, they are packed in crates, and shipped to slaughter. Fully conscious turkeys are hung upside down by metal shackles. They suffer from pain, and terror, as they are carried on a conveyor belt to where their throats are cut. They are not stunned, and as a result, hens and toms are bled to death while fully conscious. The killing methods are not precise, so many sentient turkey individuals go into tanks of boiling water while still alive.

Foie Gras is produced from hens, drakes and ganders (ducks and geese) who are a few months old. These unfortunate individuals are confined in dark sheds, and force fed large amounts of food several times a day. A worker grabs the hen, drake or gander, and forces a metal pipe down his or her neck. Then a mechanized pump shoots a mixture of corn and oil directly into their throat and stomach. This is done for a few weeks, during which time many birds die from ruptured, punctured throats, burst stomachs, and other ailments. They are dehydrated because they are not given sufficient water. In addition, they are often debeaked by a hot blade cutting through bone, cartilage, and soft tissue without any pain relief to prevent stressed individuals from injuring each other in unhealthy, crowded conditions.

The birds' enlarged livers are sold as a 'gourmet' food item after a horrific slaughter. Foie gras production is banned in the United Kingdom, Austria, Czech Republic, Denmark, Finland, Sweden, Norway, Poland, Switzerland, and Israel.

This 'gourmet protein' should be banned in the United States and other nations.

Cattle are classified as Heifers - young virgin girls, Cows – mothers, Bulls – boys, and Steers – boys who have been castrated. They are often born and live their entire lives on ranches completely unprotected from inclement weather. Thousands of individuals die because ranchers do not think it is economical to provide shelter, or veterinary care to injured, ill or otherwise ailing individuals. These unfortunate individuals have holes painfully punched in their ears for identification tags. These tags have numbers, not names. Cattle are branded with hot irons, which is extremely painful and traumatic. There is no pain relief or infection prevention administered. Cows and bulls are often transported for hundreds or thousands of miles. By law, they are allowed to travel for up to 36 hours without any food or water.

Thousands of these individuals raised for unhealth human 'protein' die every year from overcrowding, stress and disease. At stockyards and auctions, frightened individuals are kicked or shocked, and sold to the highest bidder. From there they go to slaughter or a feedlot. Younger heifers and bulls spend the last few months of their lives ingesting growth hormones and being fed an abnormal diet designed to produce fast growth. Unfortunate sick and diseased individuals are common in these filthy places.

Small planes flying overhead can smell the stench from high above the feedlots. At slaughter, conditions make it nearly impossible to treat the sentient beings with any semblance of dignity. They are often fed plastic in the days before slaughter to prevent normal defecation and the resulting clean-up. This further depletes them before their horrific deaths. Workers in slaughterhouses report hearing heart wrenching screams at slaughter. Although cattle are covered by the Human Slaughter Act, it is seldom enforced, and the resulting 'protein' is never free of the results of these horrific acts.

If you are not convinced, watch the movie 'Cowspiracy'.

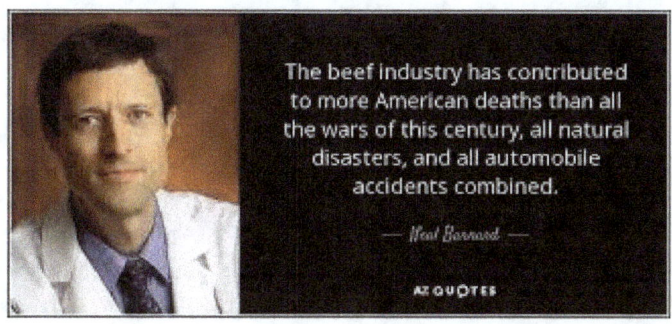

"The beef industry has contributed to more American deaths than all the wars of the century, all the natural disasters, and all the automobile accidents combined." Neil Barnard, M.D.

Chapter 16
Meet the Sea Individuals

Oceans cover more than 70 percent of the Earth's surface. About 97 percent of the Earth's water can be found in the oceans. These oceans, as well as rivers, lakes and ponds are filled with individuals we have never met, but just like us, they have feelings, families, and lives!

Today's oceans are filled with plastic and other garbage from the invasive human species, and are being over-fished to the extent that soon there will be no sea individuals left! The remaining parasites, algae, and plankton usually eaten by sea individuals, can produce toxic poisonous chemicals that cause diarrhea, paralysis, dizziness, and even memory loss in humans. When the sea individuals are all gone to be human 'protein' this is what will be left.

Fish and 'sea food' caught in the wild are killed in the most horrific, inhumane ways. Often nets that are miles long are used. These nets catch and kill many untargeted individual fish, who are just in the wrong place, at the wrong time. There are no regulations to insure humane treatment of fish. Fish plants in the U.S. make no effort to stun fish. Fish are completely conscious when they are cut. They convulse in pain as they die.

Oceans becoming exhausted and depleted have caused more than 40% of all sea individuals consumed by humans for 'protein' to be incarcerated on 'aqua farms'. These unfortunate sea individuals spend their entire lives in cramped, filthy, diseased enclosures. They suffer from parasites, diseases, and injuries. The United Nations Food and Agriculture Organization reports that the aquaculture industry is growing three times faster than land-based animal agriculture. These unhealthy, inhumane conditions breed disease for the humans who see these individuals as 'protein'.

If you are not convinced, watch the movie, 'Seaspiracy'.

BREAKING

ARGENTINA BECOMES THE FIRST COUNTRY IN THE WORLD TO BAN SALMON FARMING

Chapter 17
Food's Humble Beginnings:
Lessons in Creativity, Imagination and Resourcefulness

Ingredients for Ratatouille on the left and ingredients for Onion Soup in the center.

It is time to re-think "protein". You can do it - I will help you!

Food has humble beginnings! Have you ever thought about the elegant and sophisticated culinary works of art you so admire? Are they something you would find challenging to do yourself? Do they sometimes seem unattainable?

Take heart! Many of the now sophisticated and impressive works of culinary masterpieces were once imaginative ways to frugally prepare a nourishing meal using very simple available and affordable ingredients, with the minimum amount of costly energy.

For example, the oriental wok, now considered a culinary necessity, was originally designed to pragmatically use the smallest amounts of oil and fuel for economic reasons. Now they are seen as a much-needed culinary tool which causes the least loss of vitamins, minerals, and flavor, by those who have no need to economize.

The popular French Onion Soup started, no doubt, as a way to make something very common – the ordinary onion – into a filling, delicious and desirable meal. Although it is currently a first course, it does not take much imagination to believe that it was once a hearty and delicious main meal in more frugal times.

From personal experience, I can attest to this. One evening when I had been too busy to go food shopping, I did not have anything planed or available for dinner. But I did have an onion! It was not just any onion. It was the most beautiful locally grown onion I have ever seen! I had no plans for it when I bought it, but I just loved the way it looked, and I could not resist buying it

I knew what to make for dinner – onion soup from that onion. It was delicious and filling! I added a slice of toast for the perfect finishing touch! There was enough for the next day, and plenty for the freezer. I have no doubt that this is how the classic French onion soup started - making a delicious nutritious meal out of practically nothing. using simple available ingredients.

Another French classic – Ratatouille – was originally a stew of readily available and affordable local vegetables, cooked all day over the lowest, most economical flame, to provide a hearty and economical meal in the evening. It is now a classic with many complicated and exotic recipes available

There are countless other examples, but the point is – you do not need fancy, expensive ingredients, or complicated recipes. The most important ingredients are your own imagination, and the courage to try new things.

The first thing you want to do is to become *creative*! Forget the old meat, vegetables, and potatoes or rice, three-part formula for dinner. This paradigm is completely unfounded as a scientific or any other fact.

A balanced diet consists of protein, carbohydrates, vitamins, minerals, and fiber. It all comes from plants! Any combination is acceptable, as long as there is variety. If this new way of life is too difficult for you at first, start with vegan plant-based substitutes for meat, fish, and chicken. This will help you feel comfortable in the beginning of your journey to healthy eating. There are even plant-based meatless balls to put in your pomodoro, basil, or marinara spaghetti sauce. 'Protein' is not missing in a plant-based diet.

Cheese is not a stumbling block. You can use "cheeze" slices to make grilled sandwiches which are delicious. "Cheeze" even comes in shredded form as well as slices. There is delicious "Chezecake" in the freezer of your supermarket. This does not have to be difficult or unappetizing. It is the beginning of a new adventure!

Don't be afraid to use your own *imagination*! The worst that can happen is you that don't try that again! You may even create your own masterpieces that you and your family can come to love and treasure for generations! And if not, you can always give it to the dog. They love people food, even the rejects. But I don't think that will happen. The doggie will have to eat carrots for a snack.

Learn to be *resourceful*! Everything does not have to be perfect. The most important thing is that you try and keep trying. Enjoy your new journey of healthy and sustainable protein.

Chapter 18
Raw Food for Strength and Endurance

BUDJARGAL BYAMBAA
RAW VEGAN ULTRA LONG-DISTANCE
RUNNER

What is raw food? It is food which has not been cooked, leaving all the vitamins, minerals, and nutrients still whole and intact. Raw food is most commonly found in salads, raw fruit, uncooked vegetables - often referred to as crudites. Your grapefruit with breakfast, side salad with lunch, and uncooked vegetables at dinner all count! Raw food includes sea vegetables, nuts, seeds, sprouts, fruits, vegetables, and greens.

Many people choose to eat all their food raw. This gives the health benefits of as many vitamins, and minerals and as much fiber as possible in their diet for optimal health benefits. If you are skeptical about the raw food idea, consider this:

Budjargal Byambaa, the Mongolian vegan long- distance runner, is one of the most capable and accomplished multi-day runners in the world. He wins races all over the world that are as long as ten days in duration and the equivalent of 29 marathons! He is an ultradistance runner who runs extreme distance events over several days covering enormous distances at impressive speeds. Where does he get his protein? Raw fruit and vegetables! He is a raw food vegan!

In 2021 Budjargal ran 477 miles at Live at the Fair Running Festival, to take Gold. Later that year he took the course record at

the six-day Milwaukee Dome, with a 903
km run. Budjargal participated in the Icarus
Florida Ultrafest six-day race in 2020, and
took first place with a run of 787 km.

The ten-day Sri Chimnoy race is the
equivalent of almost 29 standard marathons.
Budjargal completed the 10-day Sri
Chinmoy race five times. He won it in 2017
(1189 km) and in 2019 (1222 km)! In 2019,
Budjargal won the Xiamen 6-day race, with
a distance of 834 km! He led second place
by 132 km, beating his own record by 17
km. In 2013 Budjargal broke the 24 hour
national record for his home nation of
Mongolia after completing 182 km.

Budjargal ran from Ulaanbaatar, Mongolia to
Beijing, China – 1500 km – within one month
to symbolize that Mongolia would win gold
medals at the Beijing Olympics.

Budjargal was born in 1982 in the South Gobi
Desert, Mongolia. He graduated from high
school in 2000, the Mongolian Defense
University in 2004, and from Ider University
in 2019.

Budjargal Byambaa is a raw food vegan who eats nothing but raw fruits, vegetables, and nuts. Budjargal stopped eating all animal products in January 2019. He was motivated by thoughts of improving his athletic performance.

"I met a doctor", Budjargal explained. "She told me that naturally suited food for the human body is not animal related food, it is plant- based food."

Now, he eats a lot of raw food, with fruit and nuts making up most of his diet. During the amazing Icarus Florida Ultrafest run he ate a lot of avocados and bananas and some nuts. He also ate coconut meat, grapes, oranges, mandarins, apples, kiwi, berries, pears and mangoes. Instead of water he drank coconut juice from a local farm, which ensured it was fresh.

"Veganism is the right choice for me, it improves my physical strength" he says. "It helps me to transcend my physical self, moving to the next stage of my spiritual development and growth."

"Long distance running is different than any other type of running. It needs not only physical strength, it needs my inner strength. My thought about inner strength is, it is so powerful, and it can give me much, much more strength than the physical strength. Becoming vegan helped me to find my inner strength."

I had the opportunity to have Budjargal Byambaa visit me and stay for a week. He told me he was a descendent of Genghis Kahn.

This is what I learned: Bud likes lemons, avocados, bananas, medjool dates, coconut meat, diced beets, apples, ginger and berries. He brought his own finely chopped beets in a kimchi jar. He also brought coconut pulp imported from Italy but bought in Chicago.

Budjargal brought lots of equipment with him! He juices peeled lemons, and peeled ginger. He adds agave and makes a drink.

He takes the lemon and ginger pulp and puts it in a jar with filtered water. What a busy place my kitchen became!

He juiced a pineapple and saved the pulp. He drank the pineapple juice, juiced a watermelon, saved pulp. and juice. He added water to the pulp and put it in jars. The chopped beets he kept in the freezer. He used plenty of water, but I never saw him drink plain water.

He believes that the chemicals in commercial soaps are detrimental to the skin and avoids it. His belief is that people should only use soap and shampoos that are edible.

Bud made a dinner casserole of blueberries, peeled, diced apples, chopped beets, pineapple pulp, ginger pulp, raisins and nuts. It was very attractive, delicious, and filling. Another casserole Budgargal made had diced squash, onions, red peppers, chopped beets, chopped parsley, blueberries, diced apples, raisins and nuts. It was also delicious!

While I was eating only fruit – specifically, whatever Bud ate – at first, I did not feel hungry; then second, although I am a vegan and in relatively good health, I began to feel even better, and some minor health issues improved significantly. I secretly retained some old habits – mostly coffee - and felt like I lost some of the progress I had made. I still do not give up the coffee!

It was an interesting experience having a raw vegan athlete guest! I took Budjargal to the ocean and lent him one of my boogie boards. I gave him the larger one. Would you believe it was his first time in the ocean! We both agreed that seeing a man in the parking lot with a fish he had just caught was totally unacceptable.

Another fun thing Bud and I did was to visit the Society of the Four Arts Sculpture Gardens in Palm Beach, which is beautiful and free- a winning combination. Bud was much more interested in Mar-A-Lago, Donald Trump's residence. I pulled over and let him get out and take pictures.

We walked in the local nature preserves, and he attended Church with me dressed up for the occasion in his white brocade suit.

Probably one of the highlights of his visit was the birthday celebration for Budjargal's 39th Birthday. He even videoed it! It must be available for view somewhere in cyber space. His visit was a wonderful and interesting experience!

Chapter 19

Adventures in Produce Shopping

WOW! LOOK AT ALL THAT!

Think of your visit to the produce market as an adventure - an opportunity to try new things and explore new possibilities. Don't go with preset ideas. Flexibility and the courage to try new things are key. Buy whatever appeals to you at the moment. Opportunities to try new things will always present themselves. Keep in mind that you need a variety of fruit and vegetables. Don't forget your old favorites, but have the courage to push the envelope. You can always go back if you forgot something or need more of something. You will only need the Supermarket for plant milk, plant butter and a few other things. Your food budget will be a fraction of what the sentient being "protein" crowd spends! Use the left-over cash to buy yourself a gift – you deserve it for being good to yourself, and to others of all species and the planet!

Chapter 20:
A Field Trip to the Supermarket

Left to Right: First Row: Lightlife Vegan 'Bacon', Oatmilk Coffee Chip Non-Dairy Ice Cream, Planet Oat Plant Milk, Follow Your Heart Vegan Mayo Second Row: Gardein Meatless Balls, Tofurkey Deli Slices (for sandwiches), Plant Butter, Hummus in two flavors. Front: Non-Dairy Cream Cheese and Follow Your Heart Non-Dairy Cheese.

Today we will take a virtual trip to the Supermarket and review the choices available. The vast majority of the products in the Supermarket is considered to be processed food – food that is in a box or bag rather than food from a tree or field – and should be avoided. Our food should be fruit, vegetables, and grains and come from Produce Markets. However, you may still need a few things from the Supermarket.

Let's start in the Dairy Department. I know there is nothing as offensive as the entire dairy industry, but you may want some substitutes while you are adjusting to a new regime, and the Dairy Department is where you will find some of them.

Non-Dairy Cream 'Cheese'. If you liked to have bagels and cream cheese in the past, you will love non-dairy cream cheese. Look for it with all the other products. A good brand is Kite Hill. This company donates to charities, and always makes delicious products. There are other brands of non-dairy cream cheese as well. Try them and see which one you like best.

Plant Butter. Now is the time to stop eating unhealthful and unethical dairy butter! Luckily there are delicious alternatives. The most popular butter alternative is Earth Balance. There are several choices of Earth Balance and Smart Balance, and many other alternative products. One is called "I Can't Believe It's Not Butter". This is a less expensive alternative, and very likeable.

Non-Dairy Yogurt. Yogurt is a good source of probiotics, the good bacteria in your intestines. It is especially helpful to replace these good bacteria after taking antibiotics. No one wants to take antibiotics. However, there are times in life when a Doctor prescribes them because it is temporarily necessary. Antibiotics kill the bad and good bacteria in your body. As soon as you finish antibiotics, yogurt is the best and most economical source of probiotics. And it is delicious! Dairy and non-dairy yogurt have probiotics however, non-dairy yogurt is a far superior choice because it lacks the lactose, hormones, microbes, salmonella, pollution, squandering of scarce resources, and unimaginable cruelty inherent in dairy products. There are several popular brands including 'So Delicious' and 'Silk'.

Plant Milk. Here is where you will find lots of choices and you may want to experiment to see which ones you like best. There is almond milk, soy milk, rice milk, coconut milk and oat milk, as well as many choices of brands of each. You may want to pass on the coconut milk, because there is alleged exploitation of monkeys being used to climb trees and remove coconuts. Try the others to see what you like best. Oak milk is really delicious in coffee!

There is no one brand that is 'better' than others. Experiment and find out which brands you like best. Feel free to take advantage of sales. The most important thing to remember is that you want products that are NON-DAIRY.

Now, we will move on to the Cereal Department. This is where you will find Oatmeal. *Do not ever associate breakfast with bacon and eggs.* This is one of the biggest mistakes you can possibly make.

Think Oatmeal! It is delicious, nutritious, easy to make and has the extra added benefit of removing cholesterol from your body. Yes! Even if you do not eat second-hand cholesterol, your own body manufacturers it. If you eat too much fat, even plant based, your own body will be stimulated to make more cholesterol.

Oatmeal solves this problem, partially if not totally. The good news is it is delicious and easy to make. Do not use instant or quick oatmeal. Instead get one that is usually called 'Old Fashioned'. This cooks on the stove top, but here is a secret: you can also cook it in the microwave. Follow the package directions or just add the oats to water and microwave for one minute. Then you are ready to add all the fruit, berries, nuts, raisins, spices, and anything else you can think of. You can have a wonderful, healthful, delicious, filling, and cholesterol reducing breakfast!

All Supermarkets are different, but in mine the spaghetti aisle comes next. Here you will find so many pasta products which are not good choices in comparison to fruits and vegetables. But if you grew up loving spaghetti, it is okay enjoying it occasionally, especially in the beginning of a dietary transition.

The problem is the sauce. If you buy sauce in the Supermarket, there are lots of wonderful choices: Marinara, Fire Roasted Vegetables, Mushroom, Basil, Roasted Garlic and Herb, Chucky Garden, Italian Tomato, Tomato and Basil, Garden Combination, Peppers and Onions, Sauteed Onion and Garlic, Garden Harvest, Chunky Tomato, and many, many more. The most important thing to remember is do not buy anything with meat, cheese, or cream (Vodka Sauce). You will not miss other sauces and you will be just as happy with these.

Next, we will go to the Produce Department. I would not recommend buying produce here. Supermarkets tend to resell produce which has been produced in the most profit oriented unsustainable manner possible. However, this is where they have refrigerated cases of interesting products. If you are newly trying to get your protein from plants, not animals, it may be difficult to do this all at once in one big step. You may be so accustomed to the second-hand protein products that you may miss them. This is normal, and not a problem.

There are wonderful plant-based meat substitutes available for you to enjoy as you continue to increase the amounts of fresh fruits and vegetables in your life. The transitionary aids include Tofurky Deli Slices for sandwiches. Tofurky is a very good company, and the products are delicious. The choices are hickory smoked, peppered, and plain. Another brand is 'Lightlife Deli Slices'. Do not buy 'Field Roast' products which you will find here. This is a slaughter company trying to profit from the compassionate as well as the exploitative contemporary market.

Non-dairy cheese is also usually in the Produce Department refrigerated cases. 'Follow Your Heart' and 'Daiya' are good brands. But I am sure there are other brands in other locations. Non-dairy cheese comes in all the usual flavors: American, Mozzarella, Parmesan, Cheddar, and all the usual forms: slices, grated, etc.

Another wonderful idea is to substitute things you may have previously loved, like second- hand protein from bacon, which is very popular and extremely inhumane, for something much better: 'Lightlife Smart Bacon'! This product is completely plant based and really delicious. I still enjoy BLTs but with this plant-based substitute and it is SO GOOD!!!

Non-dairy mayo is in this area. 'Hellmann's' makes a delicious vegan mayo, but it is not always available. 'Follow Your Heart' makes several choices of 'Vegenaise'. I use one, but I am sure they all are good. Frankly, I think they are not only more healthful, but they are definitely more delicious.

The Frozen Food section is last. Yes, this is where the ice cream is! But before we do that, let's look at what else is there. There are plethoras of meat substitutes. These include Meatless Meatballs for the spaghetti and meat ball crowd. 'Gardein' is a popular brand. The Meatless Meatballs taste just like the original but without the cruelty. Other products include 'Chic'kn', which is remotely similar to what it pretends to be. There are many other innovative products. Just be sure it is labeled **vegan** not veggie, because the latter usually contains dairy. Boca Burgers are good to have in the freezer for those times when you are hungry and do not feel like making anything. They can go under the broiler and in no time you have a fast dinner. Make sure you get the 'Original Vegan'.

Yes, now it is time for the best which was saved for last – Ice Cream. I have never seen anything so obscene as the ice cream area of a supermarket. It takes about 16 gallons of milk to make one gallon of ice cream. Every drop of that milk belonged to a Baby stolen from a Mother, and in many cases murdered for that milk. It is heartbreaking as well as infuriating to be in an ice cream deartment.

However, that does not mean that we should be deprived of enjoying something that we grew up loving. So Delicious and Oatly makes delicious non-dairy ice cream. There is Talenti Dairy Free Sorbetto. Ben and Jerry's, Haagen Dazs, and Breyers have non-dairy versions of ice cream now. Those are all delicious and cruelty free.

Do not buy any lactaid products. The name indicates that a hormone has been eliminated from the product, but all the other negativity remains. This is a dairy product full of everything we want to avoid. *It is not a non-dairy product.*

I hope this has been helpful. Although the majority of what we eat should come from Farmers Produce Markets, we grew up with food that has become a big part of our lives, and we need to be gentle on ourselves as we make the changes necessary for our health and the health of our planet.

Chapter 21
Breakfast – The Beginning

Tofu scramble with tomatoes and parsley, whole wheat toast with plant butter, coffee with or without plant milk, VEGAN 'bacon'.

The day begins with breakfast, which sets the pace for the rest of the day. Its importance cannot be over emphasized. When I visited relatives in Sweden years ago, their breakfast was the equivalent of an American lunch. I did not need a mid-morning snack as I had at home. I was totally satisfied until lunch.

Please do not ever associate bacon and eggs with breakfast. This is one of the biggest mistakes the secondary 'protein' crowd makes!

Think oatmeal! Oatmeal is famous for facilitating the removal of excess cholesterol from the human body. Even plant-based individuals occasionally have cholesterol issues if they become too fond of plant-based butters and oils. Oatmeal is extremely beneficial for those people transitioning away from the secondary protein meat and dairy based diet and struggling with cholesterol issues.

There must be at least 365 ways to prepare the never boring, always exciting, oatmeal breakfast! My favorite is 'everything'. I use everything I can find in the kitchen – blueberries, strawberries, blackberries, raspberries, bananas, kiwis, peaches, apricots, apples, pears, nuts, raisins, etc. Some combinations become favorites: blueberries, strawberries, and bananas; bananas and nuts; apples, raisins and cinnamon, and many more. Adding maple syrup or molasses provides additional sweetness. Any combination you create makes a delicious, refreshing, satisfying and never boring breakfast.

Occasionally there is a shortage of choices, but even with a limited selection – oatmeal is never boring. Apples are great in the Autumn and can be dressed up by adding raisins and cinnamon. Apples have the added benefit of longer shelf life, and are a good backup when things come up in life which supersede food shopping. Bananas alone can become more fun with added chopped nuts. Oatmeal with pumpkin puree is fabulous, and nutmeg, cinnamon, ginger and ground cloves (aka pumpkin pie spice) make it even more delicious. I never had oatmeal alone, but that might be delicious with molasses, a good source of vitamin B.

The more elegant brunch entrée, loved by even those guests, friends and family who continue to follow the secondary protein diet, is Tofu Scramble! This is delicious, and everyone, even my adult non-vegan children, love it! Your guests will too!

You will need a block of firm tofu, vegetables: peppers of as many colors as possible, onions, mushrooms, parsley, and whatever vegetables and ingredients you want to experiment with, salt and pepper, soy sauce and hot sauce if you like extra zip.

Wash and cut the vegetables, sautee in a wok or frying pan. To avoid using excessive oil, use a cooking spray. There are many available, but I prefer to use the canola oil spray. Canola oil is recommended by Neal Barnard, M.D., Founder of Physicians Committee For

Responsible Medicine. Start with the onions, then the peppers, and the mushrooms. When everything looks almost ready, add the rinsed, crumbled tofu, the soy sauce, and hot sauce to taste. Cook until all ingredients are hot.

I am sure your brunch guests will love it, and if not, the next time you invite them, they may suggest taking you out! A win-win! But I don't think that will ever happen. I think they will love whatever you create, especially the tofu scramble!

Chapter 22
Soup First

Left to Right: Pea Soup with Potatoes and Carrots, Onion Soup with Whole Wheat Croutons, Lentil Soup with Basmati Rice and Curry

The secret to weight control and weight loss: eat soup first before meals to satisfy hunger. There are many different kinds of soup, some easy and some more challenging. The most important thing to remember is never use beef or chicken stock if called for in a recipe. Always use vegetable stock, vegetable bouillon, or water. It will be just as tasty, and much more healthful.

Some favorite soups are: bean soups of all kinds: black beans, pinto beans, red beans, lentil soup, pea soup, either alone or with rice, barley, onion, carrots, celery, potatoes, etc. and vegetable soup. Soup has endless possibilities. Each culture has its own take on soup. Here are some easy and diverse recipes to try:

Classic Vegetable Soup: There are countless ways to make it. I am sure you will find your own favorite. Start with some basic root vegetables: onions, carrots, potatoes, you can include the parsnips, and whatever else you want to add. Herbs, usually parsley, can be added at the end. Start by sauteing the vegetables in cooking spray in a large soup pot. Add boiling water, vegetable stock, or bouillon. Simmer until ready. Add parsley or other herbs when finished. Experiment and use your imagination. This is fun and delicious!

Classic Bean Soup: This is a good source of protein. Grains or rice, and vegetables, add increased nutritional content. Dry beans need to be rinsed and soaked. Add beans to water and soak according to directions on the package. Large black beans can be soaked overnight. Small beans, lentils and split peas can be cooked after rinsing without being soaked. Bring water to a boil and simmer until the beans are soft. Add vegetables during the last few minutes of cooking and add herbs when finished. Use your imagination or research recipes.

French Onion Soup: This is easy and delicious, but it takes a long time. Cut onions into slices and sautee in canola spray. Wait until the onions caramelize. This takes a long time! Stir occasionally while waiting. Don't let them burn while waiting. Boil water and add to the pot when the onions have caramelized. Let the soup simmer. You can add salt and pepper if you like. Onion soup is traditionally served with toast or croutons and melted cheese. Do not use dairy cheese! It is even more delicious and healthful with non-dairy cheese slices or shreds. You must use an oven proof soup bowl if you put it under the broiler to melt. If you do not have an oven proof bowl, just add toast and non-dairy cheese. Enjoy! It is delicious and so filling!

Italian Minestrone Soup: This is a classic vegetable soup with an Italian flare – add some previously cooked pasta, and some cooked beans in a standard vegetable soup. You may want to add some oregano or Italian Seasonings for an authentic taste.

Japanese Miso Soup: This is made from dashi stock and miso paste which can be purchased in the supermarket. Miso is often considered to have health benefits from probiotics, but I think it is popular because it is delicious. It often includes sea vegetables. You can purchase both miso and sea vegetables in the Supermarket. Add boiling water to the purchased miso and rehydrate the sea vegetables in the soup. There are many people who strongly believe in the healing powers of miso, but I like it because it is delicious.

African Peanut Soup: This is really fabulous! It is basically a vegetable soup with lots of tomatoes and chunky peanut butter. Start by sauteing chopped onions, garlic which can be put through a garlic press or diced, peeled, and chopped fresh ginger. Add chopped peanuts, vegetable broth, chopped tomatoes and chunky peanut butter. Simmer. Add cut cilantro before serving. You can experiment on your own or research recipes. This is one not to be missed!

American Butternut Squash Soup: This is much easier when your local produce market sells chunks of fresh butternut squash. Otherwise, it can be a challenge to cut up the rock-hard butternut squash, but it is doable. Sautee the squash chucks and some chopped onions is a little canola oil, add some plant milk and then blend in a blender with Autumn seasonings.

Spanish Gazpacho: This is a tasty tomato-based vegetable soup which is served cold. It has tomatoes, cucumbers, peppers, red onions, and balsamic or red wine vinegar. There are countless recipes for it, and with a little experimentation, you will find one that you love. It is so refreshing in the summer before lunch or dinner!

Chapter 23
Salads: Verdant and Versatile

Salad; Radicchio, red leaf lettuce, radishes, red peppers, tomatoes. Cole Slaw: shredded cabbage, vegan mayo, clear vinegar. Potato Salad: steamed, cooled red potatoes, onions, celery, peppers, vegan mayo, clear vinegar. Jars: artichoke hearts, red and yellow roasted peppers, balsamic vinegar, black olives, green olives.

We are all familiar with the standard lettuce and tomato salad. However, there are countless ingredients you can use in salads.

Do not ever use eggs, tuna or other 'protein' that originated from a sentient being.

Any raw vegetable can be used in a salad. You may want to purchase cans or jars of ingredients such as marinated artichokes, roasted red peppers, olives, or other ingredients to have them available to add to the fresh ingredients for variety.

Refreshing Cole Slaw, Macaroni Salad, or Potato Salad are lunchtime favorites and there is no reason to change that now. The only thing that changes is the mayo. These can be made easily and tastily with Vegenaise or Hellmann's Vegan Mayo, which are really fabulous, instead of the unhealthful alternative, and clear or apple cider vinegar. Leftovers will be good the next day also.

Coleslaw is just cabbage that is grated on a grater. A grated carrot may be added. Then add vegan mayo and clear vinegar for a wonderful side of coleslaw.

Potato and macaroni salad involves steaming the potatoes or simmering the pasta (usually elbow macaroni, but you can use other forms of macaroni). Cool them in the refrigerator or freezer for a few minutes. Then add chopped onions, green peppers, carrots or whatever else you like. Finally, add the vegan mayo and clear vinegar, chill and enjoy!

Chapter 24
What's For Lunch?

Top down: Vegan Grilled Non-Dairy Cheese (whole wheat bread, plant butter and vegan non-dairy cheese); Macaroni Salad (made with Vegan Follow Your Heart Mayo, or Hellmann's which makes vegan mayo also) macaroni, onions, peppers, parsley; 'Toona' salad sandwich on whole wheat bread with tomatoes ('Toona' salad is made with hearts of palm, onion, celery, and vegan mayo); corn (served raw or grilled with a little plant butter.).

You do not have to give up the things you love to eat in order to get your protein from plants. You already love, or at least tolerate, salads and now you can enjoy some absolutely scrumptious sandwiches.

If you like tuna, you will love 'toona'. All you do is purchase a can of hearts of palm in the supermarket. Just drain it, put it in a bowl, add some chopped onions and celery, and whatever else you normally add.

This is the important part: use non-dairy mayo. There are several choices in the supermarket. Vegenaise by Follow Your Heart has several varieties, and Hellmann's has Vegan Mayo. These are much more delicious than conventional mayonnaise. They taste fresher, and there is no disagreeable aftertaste.

Another good choice is grilled non-dairy cheese. Again, 'Follow Your Heart' has several choices of non-dairy cheese. They have mozzarella, American, pepper jack, and parmesan.

All you need to do is take two slices of your favorite bread, spread plant butter on one side of each, put the non-dairy plant cheese in the center, add tomato slices if you wish, and put in frying pan. Turn over when ready, and voila, magnificent grilled cheese.

Did you think you had to give up BLTs? No, you do not! You can buy the most scrumptious plant-based products including 'SmartBacon' which is 100% plant-based and tasty, in the supermarket. Put a few slices in a frying pan with a little cooking spraying for a few minutes while your bread is toasting. Just add the vegan mayo, lettuce and tomato, and have the most mouth-watering, healthful, and compassionate 'BLT' you have ever had in your life.

Cole Slaw, Macaroni Salad, Potato Salad are lunchtime favorite sides, and there is no reason to change that now. The only thing that changes is the mayo. You will use Veganaise or Vegan Mayo now instead of the unhealthful alternative.

These sandwiches and salads can be packed up to take to work or enjoyed at home on weekends or whenever.

Chapter 25
Dinner- An Adventure in Innovation and Imagination

Grilled Portobello Mushrooms, Dairy-Free Mashed Potatoes, Sauteed Kale

This is the perfect time to push the envelope and explore new options. My favorite dinner, and maybe it will be yours, too, is Portabella Mushroom Steaks with Gravy, Mashed Potatoes made with plant milk and plant butter, and Sauteed Spinach or Kale.

This is my favorite dinner from Rosetta's Kitchen in Asheville, North Carolina. Although I do not have Rosetta's (yes, there really is a Rosetta) recipe, here are some good ones:

Mushroom Gravy:

2 cups of vegetable broth

¼ cup of red cooking wine (Cooking wine is found in the cooking aisle, not the liquor aisle in the supermarket, and is extremely inexpensive compared to drinking wine.),

½ cup of chopped onion

2 garlic cloves chopped

1 tablespoon of soy sauce

1 ½ cups of sliced portobello mushrooms

¼ teaspoon thyme leaves

¼ teaspoons of sage

1 ½ tablespoons of cornstarch mixed with 1/3 cup of water

pepper to taste.

Sautee the onion and garlic in 3 tablespoons of water, stirring often, until soft, about 5 minutes. Add mushrooms and cook until they begin to release their juices, about 10 minutes. Add broth, wine, soy sauce, thyme and sage and simmer for 10 minutes. Mix cornstarch and water in small bowl, stir into the sauce and simmer, stirring often, until slightly thickened, about 10 minutes. Season with pepper and serve.

Mashed Potatoes: Peel, or don't peel, the potatoes. Small red potatoes are great for this. Cut into pieces that are about 2 or 3 inches in diameter, and steam until soft. Reserve the cooking water. Put potatoes in a bowl with plant butter, plant milk to moisten, and mix with a mixer until there are no lumps. Serve hot with plant butter. Reserved cooking water is a good source of vitamins and can be chilled and used in cooking or just drink it.

Portobello Mushrooms: Rinse, and broil whole mushroom caps. Cook under the broiler until ready.

Sauteed Spinach or Kale. Rinse fresh spinach or kale. Remove any stems. Spray frying pan with canola oil spray. Add spinach or kale. Stir slightly until wilted and hot. Serve immediately.

With the plethora of plant-based cookbooks out there and the ubiquitous use of google, I am sure it will not be long before you have your own favorites!

Chapter 26
Herbs and Spices -The Little Giants

Fresh Parsley, Cilantro, Basil, Dill and Sage, Pepper, Cinnamon, Ground Cloves, Nutmeg, and Ginger.

Fresh bouquets of parsley, cilantro, basil, dill, those dark green pungent little guys in the Produce Market may be calling you. Answer their call! Purchase some parsley, curly or flat, cilantro, basil, dill or whatever is calling you! You will not regret it! There are no rules, although some herbs are associated with certain food. Go ahead and make your own rules! Have no rules at all!

These interesting little guys are full of vitamins, minerals and adventure! You can follow their lead wherever they take you. They can go in salads, on cooked or raw vegetables, on sandwiches, your dinner, or wherever,

Don't forget the seasonal favorites; Pumpkin pie spice, which is really a mixture of cinnamon, ground cloves, nutmeg and ginger. This is great mixed into pureed pumpkin with brown sugar. Poultry seasoning is mixture of sage, thyme, rosemary, marjoram, and black pepper is great on your Holiday tofurky. Nutritional Yeast contains B vitamins and has a nutty, cheesy, salty flavor. It is good on pasta or whatever else you want.

You are cordially invited into a new realm of culinary exploration. Try it free style or do research, whatever is your calling. Most important – do it! Don't pass up this opportunity to expand your eating horizons and avail yourself of lots of additional nutrition. They are a must!

Chapter 27
Cooking Basics – Steam, Broil, Sautee

Cooking does not have to be difficult, time consuming, inconvenient, or stressful. It can be as easy or complicated as you want it to be. I prefer 'easy' usually and 'exotic' for guests.

We all should know by now that raw fruits and vegetables are the most healthful because all the vitamins, minerals and micronutrients are intact and available for use in our bodies through digestions. I am sure we will all keep this in mind when making our food preparation choices.

However, there are times when we may want to cook and eat the way we did it in the past. You may be happy to know that vegetables can be broiled, barbequed, and otherwise prepared similar to what you have been doing previously in your non plant-based life.

Corn on the cob or other fresh vegetables under the broiler makes a wonderful meal.

Just add a little plant butter, seasonings, salad, or whatever. Fresh vegetables on a shish kabob skewer under the broiler or on a barbeque is fabulous! Use fresh mushrooms, onions, peppers, zucchini, summer squash, and whatever else catches your eye in the produce store. Add rice, potatoes, couscous, or whatever grain you like and enjoy!

Steaming instead of boiling insures a minimum loss of vitamins and nutrients. You can use a steamer pot which has simmering water on the bottom and the vegetables on top. At the end, the water in the bottom will have collected all the lost vitamins. You can chill this water and drink it later. You will be surprised at how delicious it is!

No one fries food anymore. Most people have learned by now that all the oil involved in frying is not good for your health or your weight. People sautee now. This involves fewer calories and is just as good. Use a very little bit of plant butter in your pan.

Better yet, sautee in a little water for a fat free entrée. This is how the oil free crowd does it and their sleek and slender bodies are stunning!

Chapter 28
Around the World Without Leaving the Kitchen

Vegan Swedish Pancakes

Now we will take a culinary adventure around the world from the comfort of our own kitchen. I hope this will give you plenty of ideas to explore and the inspiration to find new ones of your own. Let's start our adventure!

 **CHINA**

This is a great idea for leftovers: vegetable fried rice! It is very easy and delicious. Anyone can make it.

It usually starts with those leftover vegetables that are still good but seem too boring to do anything with. Cook rice - either brown, long grain, jasmine, basmati, or possibly use leftovers from last night's dinner. Sautee an onion in a frying pan in a cooking spray or water. Add the leftover rice and any fresh or leftover vegetables you have available. Warm it all up and add soy sauce while it is still in the pan. Serve with Chinese mustard, extra soy sauce, and enjoy! That was easy!

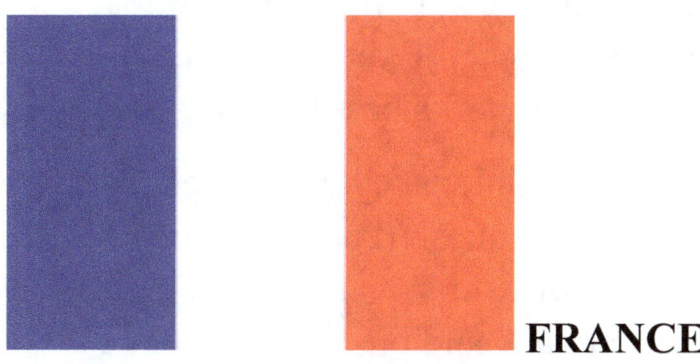 **FRANCE**

Think ratatouille! Here is a famous classic that everyone should try to make at least once in a lifetime. It is another one of those French recipes which no doubt started in an area of France which was long on imagination and creativity and short on the more finite resources. Like French Onion soup, which takes a long time.

It seems like this was possibly prepared early in the day, and then the individual worked all day while this was on the stove over a very low flame. That evening, after work, they all enjoyed a lovely vegetable stew.

There are many complicated recipes out there, but remember, this is originally a French peasant recipe, and not the gourmet situation it has become. Experiment and find the recipe that works best for you!

They all start with onions, eggplant, yellow and green summer squash (zucchini) and peppers, any or all colors. Cut the vegetables in chunks and put in a pot with a little olive oil. Let them cook for several hours over very low heat, stirring occasionally. They will reduce in size and create their own sauce. Season while cooking with your choice of salt, pepper, minced garlic, thyme, basil, fresh lemon juice, bay leaf.

This can be served over or with rice, or any other grain of your choice. Put leftovers in the refrigerator. It is often considered to be better the second day.

Voila! You are a French Chef!

HUNGARY

Budapest is one of the most beautiful cities in the world! The Danube river flows through the city dividing it into two sections: Buda and Pest. Buda is on a beautiful hill with a castle looking down on the River, and below is Pest: pronounced with a 'sh' sound instead of the English 's' sound. This was the scene of the World War II rescue of 100,000 innocent lives by one of the world's greatest heroes: Raoul Wallenberg.

Here is a delicious traditional Hungarian recipe which takes time, but like French Onion Soup, it is worth the wait!

Hungarian cabbage: Cut a cabbage into squares, about two inches by two inches, and put in a pot with a little oil. Cook until the cabbage is about half the size of the original amount. This takes time and patience.

Cut or break noodles into approximately the same 2 inches by 2 inches size. Lasagna noodles work well for this. Cook the square noodles in boiling water until soft. Combine the cabbage and noodles. Increase the heat and cook the cabbage and noodles until they are brown.

This is also great served the next day fried in a little plant butter. Leftovers can be frozen and later thawed for future easy, fast, 'comfort food' dinners! Just warm it up in a little plant butter.

 **IRELAND**

What do you think of when you think 'Irish"? St. Patrick's Day"! While you are coloring your hair and nails, and whatever else green, make you own cruelty free 'Corn Beef' and Cabbage' without the beef.

Cut cabbage in chunks, peel and cut carrots into large slices, wash and cut potatoes, peel and cut onions. Simmer water in large pot. Pierce an onion with whole cloves. Add vegetables, spiced onion, bay leaves, salt and peppercorns. Simmer all together until al dente, softened, but not mushy. Enjoy! Happy Saint Patrick's Day!

 **ITALY**

We all love pasta, and the good news is you can still enjoy it, but with plant-based protein and meatless pasta sauce.   It is still yummy.

Pasta Primavera is simply made with your favorite pasta, linguine, angel hair or whatever, simmered, drained, and served with a meatless tomato pasta sauce full of sauteed fresh vegetables of your choice. You can use fresh mushrooms, onions, peppers, or whatever you brought home from the Produce Market. Top with freshly chopped parsley, cilantro, or basil.

Spaghetti and Meatless Balls are wonderful as you remember them!. Use Meatless Balls by Gardein which are available in the freezer section of your supermarket with all

298

the other plant-based frozen foods. Choose how many of them you want, return the rest to the freezer and add to the meatless pasta sauce. They thaw out in your simmering meatless pasta sauce and taste just like the ones you remember from before you were plant-based. Cook and drain pasta, add sauce and meatless balls and optional grated non-dairy parmesan cheese.

Eggplant No Parmesan is without the cheese. or with plant-based non-dairy Parmesan. This is a new way for an old favorite. Unfortunately, the original method uses a lot of oil, so either use cooking spray, or if you do use oil, do not do it too often or you may find yourself becoming chubby.

Peel and slice the eggplant. Optional: dip in plant-milk. Sautee in cooking spray, layer in an oven proof container, top with meatless pasta sauce, sprinkle with grated non-dairy cheese from the Produce Department of the Supermarket and bake until browned. It's out of this world magnificant!

KOREA

Korea is famous for the cabbage dish, Kim Chi. It comes in many flavors and can be purchased in the supermarket. never had it, but it is on my to-do list for someday. I understand it is very popular but have not had the courage to try it yet.

MEXICO

Guacamole, Salsa, Refried Beans sound great. We all love Mexican Restaurants, but did you know you could make your own fresh and creamy guacamole and spicy salsa at home? If you follow that with refried beans and savory rice, you have a filling, healthful and festive meal which is quick and easy.

In Florida, where I currently live, many people and their neighbors have their own avocado trees. Some neighbors put them out for others to take because there is often too many for one family. People find them on lawns or wherever when they are in season. This is a great start to making inexpensive and impressive guacamole! You can also buy avocados in the produce store.

Use a ripe avocado and remove the pulp from the skin. Put the pulp in a bowl and add finely chopped onions and garlic. Cut a lemon or lime in half and squeeze both halves into your avocado mixture. Top with chopped cilantro and you have guacamole.

Salsa is a different story. This lends itself nicely to as many varieties as your imagination can think of. Usually it involves tomatoes, but I have had incredibly memorable and refreshing mango salsa also.

A basic salsa recipe involves tomatoes cut in chunks, minced garlic cloves, chopped sweet pepper, and onion, add chopped cilantro, pinch of cumin, lime juice, salt, pepper, chop a jalapeno pepper and add sparingly and taste until the right level of heat is reached.

Refried beans are filling, satisfying, and easy to make. Use a can of pinto or black beans drained. Sautee a medium chopped onion, and a few garlic cloves, with a little cumin, and a little chipotle powder in a cooking oil spray. Add half of the drained beans and half a cup of vegetable broth. Mash until creamy. Add the remaining beans and another half cup of vegetable broth, mash again. Cook over medium heat for 15 more minutes. The longer you cook it, the thicker it will be!

This all goes great with your favorite Mexican rice recipe. Enjoy! Ole!

MIDDLE EAST: *CYPRUS, ISRAEL, JORDAN, LEBANON, PALESTINE, QATAR, SAUDI ARABIA, SYRIA, UNITED ARAB EMIRATES, YEMAN*

Falafel is so exotic and so filling that one new immigre to Israel asked what kind of meat it was. It is so similar to the abhorrent and incredibly cruel hamburger that it fooled a meat eater! Don't let it fool you! It is chick-pea based, easy to prepare, and wonderful to experience. It comes from a supermarket or middle eastern store in a box. Just add water to the dry powder, let it rest a few minutes, shape it into balls or patties, and fry or sautee.

Israeli salad is another tasty and easy to make item. Cut up ripe tomatoes into chunks. Cut up red onions and slice a peeled cucumber. Add salt and lemon juice. It is easy, refreshing, and goes great with everything especially, falafel and rice.

Baba Ghanoush is one of the best ways to serve eggplant! Use half an eggplant and place cut side down on parchment paper over a cookie sheet. Roast in the oven until soft. Scrape the eggplant out of the skin. Put the mushy eggplant in a bowl and use a food processor or whatever else you use to make a smooth consistency. Add tahini – a fabulously scrumptious sesame product from the Middle Eastern store or supermarket - and minced garlic. Finish with juice from a fresh squeezed lemon. Mix and all ingredients and enjoy your Baba.

Use half an eggplant. Put cut side down on pan and roast in oven (400 0r 450) for about an hour or until eggplant is very soft. Cool, scoop out insides and discard skin. Let drain in colander. Mince garlic and add along with lemon juice and salt. Finally add tahini and refrigerate until ready to eat. Enjoy with humus, falafel, Israeli salad, rice for a memorable dinner or lunch.

Baba Ghanoush is a thousand times better than humus! You do not even need a blender or food processor. Just remember that lemons have seeds. You may want to squeeze your lemon into a bowl or container and remove the seeds before adding it to the eggplant. Serve it with raw vegetables or sprouts, olives, whatever suits your fancy! Enjoy!

Tahini is a product made from sesame seeds. It is my favorite on bread or crackers, in recipes like Baba, or on salads. You can buy it in Middle Eastern stores, some Produce Stores or the Supermarket.

Humus is a refreshing and nutritious Middle Eastern product made from chick-peas. You can make your own or purchase it in the store. It has become increasingly popular and comes in many flavors, including roasted red pepper, black olive, garlic, plain, spicy, and more. It is so satisfying on pita bread or anything else including salad. It is better than oily, calorie laded, nutritionally deficient salad dressing. Humus and tahini are ideal choices to replace preservative and oil laden, and nutritionally deficient commercial salad dressings.

Pita bread goes great with a Middle Eastern lunch or dinner. Again, this can be purchased in a Middle Eastern Bakery or Supermarket. Understandably, there is no comparison in the quality.

Kalamata olives go great with a Middle eastern lunch or dinner. They are available fresh in a Middle Eastern store or otherwise in the Supermarket.

Greek Salad is popular but contains feta cheese. If you order this in a restaurant, be sure to ask for it without the feta cheese.

 **RUSSIA**

Mushroom Stroganoff is a Russian classic! Close your eyes and travel back in time to the Russian Tearoom in Manhattan on a Sunday afternoon after enjoying a wonderful Saturday evening in Manhattan!

The feelings evoked are so euphoric, relaxed and sensual! These are the feelings that mushroom stroganoff will conjure up for you! You must try it! This is the vegan version. Go ahead, explore, experience and enjoy!

You will need portobello and other mushrooms, garlic, onions, rosemary, eggless pasta, non-dairy sour cream, salt and pepper, cooking wine, which is from the supermarket, not the liquor store, and is much less expensive.

Sautee the onions, garlic, salt, pepper and rosemary. Add portobello mushrooms and other mushrooms. Cook about 10 minutes. add other mushrooms and cooking wine, cook 20 minutes, add non-dairy sour cream, add cooked eggless pasta ribbons, toss, and garnish with parsley. This is a great entrée for both plant-based and others for a formal dinner in your home.

 **SWEDEN**

Swedish Pancakes are my favorite food in all the world! I grew up eating and loving Swedish pancakes! Words just cannot express how much I love them! The originals are full of dairy, so this is the

dairy-free version. I created it myself
through trial and error while remembering
the original taste, consistency, color and
nostalgia.

My Grandmother Emma Leontine Anderson
Wallenberg came from Halmstad, Sweden.
She taught my Mother how to make
Swedish pancakes. This vegan version is as
close as you can come to the original.

Start with a banana. Use about a half a
banana per person. Mash it in a bowl. This
is the egg substitute. Warm a frying pan and
melt non-dairy plant-butter in it. You will
need more plant butter than you would
consider healthful, so don't do this too often.

Put about three tablespoons of flour per
person in the bowl with the mashed banana.
Add enough plant milk to make a batter
which is not too thick or too thin. Pour the
melted plant butter from the frying pan into
the batter and stir. Add more plant butter to
the frying pan.

Pour the batter into the hot frying pan with the melted plant-butter. The time it takes to cook varies according to your frying pan. Be aware that you may have to add more plant butter if the frying pan gets too dry.

Eventually you will turn the pancake over and can add more plant-butter depending on how the pancake is doing. You may need a little practice for this.

When it is finished, put on a plate, and serve hot with fresh fruit, berries, and syrup. I prefer Maple syrup but use whatever you like.

Coffee goes great with this.

One of the few things I have left from my Grandmother, Nana Leontine, is the tile she carried in her luggage when she left the Swedish port city of Malmo and entered Ellis Island in New York to start a new life. It says:

"Kaffetaren den basta ar av alla jordiska drycker"

This translates: "Coffee is the best of all the earthly drinks."

Like my Grandmother, it is my favorite too, and goes great with Swedish pancakes!

 **THAILAND**

Vegan Pad Thai is one of the fastest and easiest things you can make, and it is always a big hit with guests! Normally, Pad Thai would include an egg, but it is just as delicious and cruelty free without the egg!

You will need Pad Thai rice noodles, which you can buy in the International section of your Supermarket. Pad Thai Sauce is available in jars near the noodles. You will need to purchase fresh limes and cilantro from the Produce Store. The last ingredient is peanuts which you may already have at home.

Put the noodles in boiling water, turn down to a simmer and cook for a few minutes. Drain. Chop the peanuts and slice the limes. Put the drained noodles in a bowl and add the sauce. Stir, squeeze lime juice from some of the limes on it, and place in a serving bowl. Add the chopped peanuts and rinsed chopped cilantro on top. It only takes a few minutes to make, and you or your guests will love it!

 **UNITED STATES**

We are back home in the United States in our own kitchens, and rethinking an old favorite: Macaroni and Cheese. This is the quintessential American favorite, and in the original form, ladened with cruelty. The cruelty free version is just as heart-warming, and just as easy to make.

First, make a roux. This means you melt a little plant butter in a pan and add flour. Stir together until you have a soft ball. Then add plant milk and keep stirring until the mixture thickens. When it is thick like gravy add grated non-dairy cheese by Follow Your Heart or Dayia, which you buy in the refrigerated section of the Produce Department of your Supermarket.

Boil water and add macaroni. Cook until macaroni is al dente: soft, but still firm (not over-cooked). Drain and reserve.

While the water is coming to a boil, and the macaroni is cooking - melt a little plant butter in a saucepan. Add some flour and mix into a paste. Slowly add plant milk and dilute the paste so that it becomes a smooth liquid. Let this continue over a low heat. Continue stirring unil the mixture thickens. Add non-dairy cheese shreds and stir until melted. Combine macaroni and sauce in an oven proof container. Sprinkle breadcrumbs on top and put in the oven at 350 degrees until yummy. Serve hot!

Or you can buy a premade one by Dairea, and follow the package directions. Either way, it is just great!

Chapter 29

The Three Sisters -
Ancient Wisdom for the Digital Age

**The Three Sisters: Ancient Wisdom For
the Perfect Agriculture and the Perfect
Protein. Why Didn't We Think of That!!!**

Now we will travel back to ancient times for a lesson in wisdom. We can learn something from former civilizations about maximum nutrition and minimum work from the Three Sisters.

Ancient civilizations referred to corn, beans and squash as the Three Sisters. The wisdom of this is amazing. It was an effective, creative way of agriculture and the perfect protein and nutrition.

Corn was planted in the center of a mound and beans planted around it. Squash was planted next in an outside circle. When they grew, the corn formed a pole for the beans to climb up, and the squash put out leaves that covered the earth, preventing weeds from growing, and retaining moisture in the soil.

Not only was this as perfect agricultural plan, but it was also a perfect diet. The corn (grain) and beans (legumes) provided the perfect protein, and the squash (vegetable) provide additional fiber, vitamins, and minerals in the diet. These ancient people created a method that required less work and provided more nutrition than their modern counterparts (us) came up with.

The Three Sisters were maximum nutrition with minimum effort. Good nutrition does not have to be complicated. Protein does not need to be from other individuals.

The perfect protein of rice, beans, and vegetables has sustained civilizations for centuries. Unfortunately, this also gives it the feeling of being 'old fashioned' and associates it with being indigent or lacking sophistication. This is unfortunate but it can be overcome.

Rice and beans, the perfect protein does not have to be boring or unimaginative. It should be innovative and creative! It can be as elegant as Green Beans Almandine at the Waldorf Astoria, or as much fun as vegetables with fruit preserves and rice cooked in coconut milk served by the followers of Sri Chimnoy at their restaurant in Queens. Other popular rice and beans combos include old fashioned Succotash:

corn and lima beans, and Mexican refried beans and rice.

Here are some tasty recipes:

Beans should be rinsed before use, and some larger varieties should be soaked in water for a few hours or overnight, before cooking.

Bean Soup: Black Beans, Split Peas, Red Beans, Lentils, 6 oz. total. Bring 5 or 6 cups of water to a boil. Add Beans, cover and simmer for 2 hours. Cut up celery, carrots, potatoes. Add during last few minutes. When finished, add salt, paprika and chopped parsley.

Rice: Preheat saucepan on high for 2 or 3 minutes. Add 2 Tablespoons of oil or cooking spray and one Tablespoon of chopped garlic. Cook 1 or 2 minutes. Stir in 1 cup of rice, (Brown, Jasmine, Basmati or whatever), 1 teaspoon of cumin, ¼ teaspoon each of red pepper and salt. Cook and stir 2 – 3 minutes. Pour in 2 Cups of vegetable stock or bouillon. Bring to a boil,

reduce heat, cover. Cook 18 to 20 minutes
until the rice is tender. Enjoy!

Chapter 30
The Four Seasons

Produce: Fruit, vegetables, and grains are seasonal. That means they are never boring and always spontaneous!

Think of seasonal produce like the elegance of New York's Four Seasons restaurant, or the magnificence of Vivaldi's Four Seasons. Seasonal produce is an opportunity for you to reorganize the way you think about protein, much the same way as Vivaldi reorganized the orchestra into an innovative musical tableaux about the cycle and alternation of the seasons each with its own characteristics.

Seasonal produce gives you an opportunity to explore a kaleidoscope of plant-based protein much like the musical tableaux about the cycle and alternation of the seasons, each with its own characteristics. As the seasons change, you have the opportunity to enjoy new offerings at the Produce Store. Plant-based protein is never boring!

Spring, is the season of new life, like the phoenix rising from the ashes, and time to enjoy baby green salads and fresh vegetables picked before reaching maturity early in the season.

Summer's hot weather is the best time to enjoy barbeques of fresh *r*oasted corn on the cob with a salad of freshly picked tomatoes. Vegetable Shish Kabobs are so easy to prepare, and so attractive, with skewers of fresh mushrooms, onions, zucchini, yellow summer squash, and peppers, roasted and served over rice. It is Ratatouille time, and time to explore many other interesting and imaginative summer creations.

Autumn is the season of harvest, falling leaves, bright blue weather and pumpkins! Pumpkins are not only decorative, but they make the best pies, using soft tofu – not eggs, and pumpkin pudding using pumpkin puree, brown sugar and spice. Butternut Squash Soup is a seasonal classic made easy with pre-cut butternut squash squares from the Produce Market, sauteed, mashed and simmered with water or vegetable bouillon, and seasonings.

*Winte*r is the last of the seasons and a good time to enjoy the juxtaposition of cooler weather with the warmth of rock-hard winter squash baked soft in the oven. Spaghetti Squash may be cut in half, baked cut side down, the stringy pulp scooped out, and served with pasta sauce for a low carb and delicious dinner.

Chapter 31
Dessert - Elegant Endings

Elegant Pineapple Upside Down Cake with Coffee and Plant-Milk

Cakes are always made without eggs. A good egg substitute is one teaspoon of clear vinegar and enough plant milk to make ¼ Cup per egg substituted for. Everything else is the same.

Plant-based, non-dairy desserts do not have to be boring. Here are two chocolate mousse recipes which are sweet and refreshing. There are many more recipes for you to explore. Think of it as an adventure! Enjoy!

Raw Chocolate Mousse:

½ Cup pitted medjool dates soaked in water for 10 minutes and drained

½ Cup maple syrup or agave

¾ cup mashed avocados (approximately 1 ½ avocados)

6 Tablespoons of carob powder or cocoa

¼ Cup water

Combine dates and syrup in a food processor, add avocado, and carob or cocoa powder. Process. Remove and enjoy!

Chocolate Mousse:

2 12.3 oz boxes of silken tofu

4 tablespoons of carob or cocoa powder

1 teaspoon of vanilla

1 cup of date paste

Blend tofu, carob, cacao or cocoa powder, date paste and vanilla in a blender until well blended. Chill before serving, and it will get thicker.

Date Paste:

2 Cups of Medjool pitted dates

2 cups of water

Combine the dates and water in a blender and puree until smooth. Store in the refrigerator for up to 7 days or in the freezer for up to 3 months.

Chapter 32
Holiday Menus

Holidays can be just as festive if not more so, with your plant-based, sustainable, healthful new holiday menu celebrations.

Roasts are just as festive, and just as nostalgic when they are tofurkey or other wonderful alternatives. They can have all the traditional accompaniments including fabulous gravy and stuffing, all included in your tofurkey box. Everything else can be the traditional items but the plant-based version. That means you use plant milk and plant butter in the mashed potatoes. Almost everything else can stay the same.

There are many memorable pumpkin recipes which do not use eggs or dairy milk. Pumpkin 'pudding' is easy and yummy. It is just canned pumpkin, brown sugar and pumpkin pie spice. I love the Holidays just for that favorite dessert. It is so easy and so joyful!

Chapter 33
Baking: Yes, You Still Can!

Love is always in season, not just for Valentine's Day

You do not have to give up baking! It is just as easy to substitute eggs with mashed bananas, applesauce, or plant milk and vinegar. Cakes, cupcakes, and muffins are just as good, if not better this way. And they are healthier for you!

You can use all your original recipes with a minor substitution. If you make your own frosting, you just substitute cream of tartar for any dairy ingredients. No one will ever know the difference! And they will look and taste great!

When my Grandchildren were little, all they wanted for dessert on Holidays were Grandma's cakes and cupcakes, no matter how beautiful the store-bought ones were.

I made cakes for every Holiday, and hope you enjoyed the pictures of some of them!

Chapter 34
Agriculture:
Conventional, Organic, and Veganic

Veganic
is the future of agriculture.

One of the major excuses for animal agriculture is that manure is essential for growing food crops. But many farmers are discovering that they can grow nutritious and plentiful vegetables and fruits with just the use of plant-derived compost. The future of agriculture is animal-free.

VeganStreet.com

If protein comes from plants, what kind of plants: fruit and vegetables, do we want to eat? Veganic! Consumers must make their voices heard! Ask for Veganic, not Organic, Produce!

The standard American farm model depletes fruit and vegetables of the vitamins and minerals they would normally acquire from soil by overplanting. This is what causes tasteless produce. Almost all of the elements in the Chemistry Table of the

Elements, are found in soil. These nutrients are what is needed for optimal health.

Conventional and organic agriculture have one goal: profit. Soil is not allowed to rest and replenish because the belief is that an empty field does not produce a profit. Instead, fields are repeatedly planted and harvested making heavy applications of fertilizers and pesticides necessary. This is on conventional farms and organic farms. The only difference is that organic farms use organic fertilizers and organic pesticides, which are also harmful.

Fertilizers and pesticides, even 'organic' ones, are poison, and are unnecessary in veganic agriculture. Fertilizers from animal waste found in factory farms and slaughterhouses are the cause of bacterial infestations in conventional and organic crops. This includes salmonella, E. coli, and many others. Organic animal waste comes from organic animals who have the same intestinal bacteria as non-organic animals, and people.

Organic agriculture is a method of agriculture that requires adhering to certain rules and regulations. For example, the soil cannot have been previously used for standard farming for a certain number of years. It requires extensive record keeping, which is checked on a regular basis by an Organic Certifier. Fertilizers and pesticides are allowed, just like on a commercial farm, except that only certain 'organic' products can be used. These can be just as poisonous as standard agricultural products and are used liberally.

The extra money you pay for organic produce does not cover healthful additions to the produce. It pays for the time it takes to keep the extensive records, it pays for the Certifier's time and travel expense to check the records, and finally it pays for all the fertilizers and pesticides, all of which have their own problems.

In conventional and organic agriculture, poisonous pesticides are used to kill predators. These predators become resistant to pesticides and require stronger and more poisonous pesticides. This toxicity is passed on to the consumer. Crop rotation, leaving one field empty, does not exist in Standard American Agriculture or in Organic Agriculture. It is believed to reduce profit, so it is not used. This focus on profit robs produce of valuable nutrients, and the use of pesticides increases the health hazards inherent in eating the produce.

According to experts, industrial chemical-based agriculture, conventional and organic, is one of the most destructive human activities on the planet.

Veganic agriculture is different. To maintain an acceptable level of nutrients, soil needs to be replenished between crops. Soil needs to rest and be nourished so that the next crop will have access to the vitamins and minerals which give fruit and vegetables their nutritional value and taste. Without this natural practice, it is necessary, even for organic farms, to use fertilizers to sustain the new crops. But in Veganic

Agriculture, nitrogen rich cover crops are grown, and plowed under so that the soil is enriched with nitrogen and other nutrients.

Veganic Farms use crop rotations, cover crops, and veganic (plant based) compost. Nitrogen rich cover crops are planted and then plowed under to enrich the soil without expensive and toxic fertilizers. Pesticides are not used or needed either. Instead, the crops are rotated, or planted in a different location, each growing season. By the time a predator finds the crop it is looking for, the crop has already been harvested. There is no need for expensive poisonous pesticides.

Veganic Agriculture is the most healthful, most sustainable, and most compassionate form of agriculture. It is also the most profitable. The gross income is less, because some fields are resting, but there are no expensive inputs of poisonous pesticides and fertilizers, so the net income is more. Veganic produce is full of vitamins and minerals and has no harmful pesticides and fertilizers. Veganic Agriculture uses no animal inputs. Conventional and organic agriculture use manure from slaughterhouses. Organic produce uses manure from organic animals which contains the same fecal bacteria as all animals and humans. Veganic produce has no risk of disease or antibiotic resistance from animal manure fertilizer.

Veganic produce is rich in vitamins, minerals, and flavor, and it has none of the unhealthy toxic fertilizers and pesticides used in conventional or organic agriculture. It has no hormones or antibiotics from animal manures and inputs as used in conventional and organic farming. It has a light carbon footprint, is globally sustainable, and is totally cruelty free.

Veganic agriculture is becoming more popular as the ethical, environmental, and personal health arguments for plant-based diets becomes increasingly recognized. The demand for food produced without animal inputs, expensive and unhealthy fertilizers and pesticides is expected to rise. In addition to offering truly plant-based food options to vegans and aspiring vegans, veganic agriculture has the potential to provide regenerative and agroecological solutions to leading food system issues. This includes resource depletion, environmental destruction, and foodborne illness related to animal by-products.

Currently, there is a Veganic Agricultural Network in North America which is a good resource for further information in this growing worldwide movement. In Europe it is called Stock-Free Organic, and in Asia it is called Natural Agriculture. Although there is a strong veganic agriculture movement worldwide, consumers must show retailers that there is a demand for this healthful, and sustainable agriculture. Ask for veganic, not organic, produce when you shop!

Non-Animal Input Agriculture
Growing a more resilient future and breaking the dependance on livestock/slaughterhouse wastes

Chapter 35
Let's Eat Out!

Farmers Table, Boca Raton, Florida

Eating out does not have to be challenging!
Increasingly more restaurants are serving
vegan alternatives. Be careful! Many
places do not distinguish between vegetarian
and vegan, so they use dairy cheese which
you want to avoid. Read descriptions
carefully and ask questions of your Server.

Chinese Restaurants usually have a vegetable section on the menu which includes such delicious options as Eggplant in Garlic Sauce, Buddha's Delight (tofu and vegetables), and many others. These are great, and so is Vegetable Fried Rice (*ask for it without the eggs*), Vegetable Lo Mein, Vegetable Chow Mein, and Vegetable Chop Suey, among others.

Italian Restaurants can make entrees vegan upon request. A favorite is Eggplant Parmesan without the cheese. There are plenty of pasta dishes with Pomodoro or Marinara Sauce. Your Server can also make suggestions.

Thai and Asian Fusion Restaurants have tofu entrees which are piquant and pungent. These are usually made with coconut milk, not dairy milk in the sauces. Ask your Server, just to be sure.

Mexican Restaurants have entrees like vegetable fajitas which are fresh and savory. Vegetarian burritos without the cheeses and sour cream are also amazingly satisfying.

Guacamole can be substituted for these. Salsa seems to always be meat and dairy free.

American restaurants are offering more and more veggie alternatives, but they do not distinguish between Vegetarian and Vegan. They don't seem to realize that dairy is not acceptable, and try to include cheese in everything. Ask for whatever the menu item is without the cheese.

Eating out will still be fun and although there will be a slight adjustment period, the inconvenience will be offset by the substantially lower check at the end! Have fun! Experiment! Enjoy!

Chapter 36:
My Plant-Based Vegan Kitchen

Any book about food would be remiss
without a tour of the Author's kitchen. So
here it is!

Utensils. There was no change in any utensils when changing from the old-fashioned meat and dairy based diet to vegan cuisine 20 plus years ago. I use the same knives, wooden spoons, spatula, scraper, etc. In fact, the instrument I use to turn over corn on the cob under the broiler is the same instrument that my parents used to remove my baby bottles from hot water (no comment on how many years ago). Although it does not seem like knives are necessary for a Plant-Based Lifestyle, I challenge you to try to tackle a butternut squash without a chainsaw!

The Basics. My goal is to use only Veganic produce, hopefully from my own farm someday. For now, I buy fruit, berries, and vegetables from a local produce market. I usually know what I want, like bananas, blueberries and corn on the cob. But I am also open to surprises and whatever is fresh and attractive. In addition, I buy rice (brown, jasmine, basmati, wild, etc.) depending on what is available, and what I am in the mood for. I also include lentils, split peas, chic- peas, pinto beans, black beans, etc.

Measure. I do not measure anything except oatmeal. Sorry if that is a disappointment. I usually 'wing it', and everything turns out just fine.

Oil. I use canola oil cooking spray for sauteing, but I know many people sautee in water. I do not use oil for salad or anything else except Massage (oil for receiving Massage, not eating). Balsamic vinegar, hummus or tahini are good in salad instead of oily salad dressings which are full of unnecessary calories..

Vegan Food Products. I purchase Follow Your Heart Vegenaise. I have tried Hellman's Vegan Mayo, which was great, but I have not seen it again. I use this with a little clear vinegar to make coleslaw from shredded cabbage and carrots; macaroni salad from pasta, green peppers, and onions; and potato salad from potatoes, celery, onions, and green peppers. It is so good!

Plant milk. Oat, almond, or soy milk, are delicious, and good in coffee.

Plant butter.   I use a little for broiled corn on the cob etc. and in Swedish pancakes.

Egg Substitute. For vegan cakes I use a teaspoon of clear vinegar and enough plant milk to make ¼ cup to replace one egg. It works beautifully. Everyone loves my imaginative and festive vegan holiday cakes. When my Grandchildren were small, they would only eat Grandma's vegan cakes for dessert on holidays, no matter how beautiful the store-bought desserts were! They don't do that anymore. Another good egg substitute is mashed bananas. This is just perfect in Swedish pancakes!

I had humble beginnings, and live and eat simply. Although I am completely at home at black tie events, parties in Sutton Place, the Indonesian Lounge at the United Nations, and other upscale and exotic venues, talking to United States Senators, United Nations Ambassadors, Celebrities, and more, I stay true to my humble roots at home.

Please enjoy your plant-based lifestyle experience in whatever way makes you happy. Vegan is about compassion - to yourself and others of all species! Remember if you are eating out – many vegetarian options contain milk and butter. Be careful. Most importantly – enjoy yourself!

Chapter 37 Conclusion.

Now we are at the end of our adventure in "Protein".

The lesson here is that meat, dairy, eggs, and sea animals are not a good source of "protein" for humans. Animal agriculture and aquaculture is not good for the environment. Secondary "protein" is certainly not good for those individuals seen as "protein" instead of the unique sentient individuals they really are.

All energy comes from the sun, and primary protein photosynthesized from the sun in plants – fruit, vegetables, grains and legumes - are the best source of protein for humans!

I hope these lessons in where you get your protein have been helpful, and possibly even life changing. Remember, protein comes from plants! Now it is your turn to find easy, delicious, and even exotic ways to enjoy your protein from plants. Use your imagination and enjoy yourself! Don't follow rules! Explore! Experiment! Don't be intimidated! You are cordially invited to find out what's right for you. Most importantly, enjoy yourself while making the world a better place for you, all your fellow travelers, and our very special home, spaceship Earth, where there is enough protein for all travelers if we use it wisely.

Sharon Leontine Wallenberg, Author

www.ingramcontent.com/pod-product-compliance
Lightning Source LLC
Chambersburg PA
CBHW060856120626
46553CB00001B/106